THIS BOOK
BELONGS TO:
♡ Liliana Faith ♡

January 09, 2007
Birth date:

4:57 AM
Birth time:

Holland, Michigan
Birth location:

Virgo ☾ Scorpio ♏

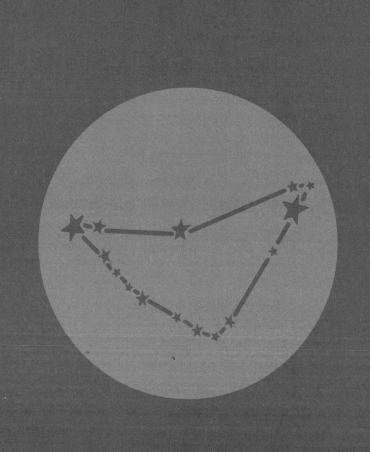

ZODIAC SIGNS

CAPRICORN

ZODIAC SIGNS

CAPRICORN

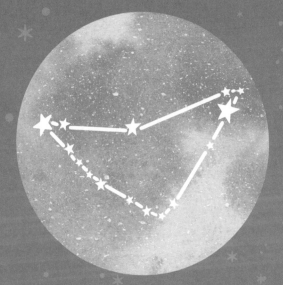

KELSEY BRANCA

STERLING ETHOS
New York

STERLING ETHOS
New York

An Imprint of Sterling Publishing Co., Inc.
1166 Avenue of the Americas
New York, NY 10036

ISBN 978-1-4549-3892-7

Distributed in Canada by Sterling Publishing Co., Inc.
c/o Canadian Manda Group, 664 Annette Street
Toronto, Ontario M6S 2C8, Canada
Distributed in the United Kingdom by GMC Distribution Services
Castle Place, 166 High Street, Lewes, East Sussex BN7 1XU, England
Distributed in Australia by NewSouth Books
University of New South Wales, Sydney, NSW 2052, Australia

For information about custom editions, special sales, and premium
and corporate purchases, please contact Sterling Special Sales at
800-805-5489 or specialsales@sterlingpublishing.com.

Manufactured in China

2 4 6 8 10 9 7 5 3

sterlingpublishing.com

Cover design by Elizabeth Mihaltse Lindy
Cover and endpaper illustration by Sarah Frances
Interior design by Nancy Singer
Zodiac signs ©wikki33 and macrovector/freepik

CONTENTS

β

INTRODUCTION

*God is a circle whose center is everywhere and
circumference is nowhere.*

—Hermes Trismegistus

Astrology is a symbol-based language of cycles and
time. It is the study of how celestial bodies, such as
planets and asteroids, and their motion through the twelve
signs of the zodiac influence life on planet Earth. Dating
back thousands of years, astrology spans many different
cultures and geographic regions. Nearly every human culture has, at one time, looked up and told stories about what
they saw in the night sky above them. Western astrology as
we know it now is an amalgamation of 2,400 years of sym-
bolic language that speaks of gods and goddesses, mythical
creatures, and archetypical wisdom.

The language of astrology can be interpreted differently, depending on cultural values, since mores affect how we choose to apply astrological insights. We can look at agriculture (based in the northern hemisphere) through the lens of astrology to see cycles of light and plant life. We can look at traditional medical practices through the lens of astrology to better understand how the planets function in the human body in health and also at the onset of disease. Using astrology, we can weave our human stories to understand change over time, for one individual or for an entire generation. We can look at the current astrological weather and how it impacts life on planet Earth. We can use astrology in conjunction with spirituality and religious philosophy to peer deep into our inner knowing and cycles of personal unfolding, yet the atheist and agnostic may also study astrology for a practical understanding of ancient archetypical language. There should be no conversation about whether or not astrology "exists": it certainly does exist—as a tool of human creation that either works for you or doesn't.

As is true for many languages, the interpretation of astrology has been influenced by colonialism and oppression.

Western astrology exists today primarily because of Roman conquests influencing common language in what are now parts of Europe, Asia, Africa, and the Middle East. Many ancient texts were destroyed as Roman and British colonizers used brute force to erase the indigenous cultures of their rivals. Astrology is a language developed by and for the ruling class, and was available only by consulting skilled astrologers. It is only in recent years that laypeople have had access to software that will instantly calculate their own natal or birth chart, providing a map of where the planets were at the time of birth. Now more than ever, people can view their natal charts, which means that taking time and care to translate accurately is important. Unskilled translation of astrology means that unfortunately the Internet is rife with astrology blogs and memes that reinforce narrowly defined and sometimes racist or sexist stereotypes that say less about astrology and more about the culture we live in. Memes are fun, but usually present simple, boring, rigid interpretations of a deeply complex language. Astrology is meant to be multifaceted and ever changing, so it is especially important to know who is behind the translation.

MYTHOLOGY: THE BIRTH OF CAPRICORN

Capricorn is one of the oldest myths, dating back to ancient Babylonian culture as the deity Ea, who was described as the "antelope of the sea." Ea is related to Enki in Sumerian mythology, the trickster god of fresh water, culture, fertility, wisdom, healing, creation, and art. Enki was one of the three major deities in Mesopotamian mythology, as well as one of the seven earliest Sumerian gods. He was portrayed with the upper body of a goat and the tail of a fish; both fish and goats were common symbols of fertility. He was also shown as an old man wearing a horned cap, climbing mountains, with water streaming down his body. Myths featuring Enki told stories about the corruption of power, sexuality and life-giving water (semen), creation and birth. Many stories of Enki are about how he brings positive change to humankind, though humans misunderstand his intentions.

CAPRICORN'S BUILDING BLOCKS: ELEMENT, MODALITY, AND POLARITY

Each of the twelve members of the zodiac can be described by their element, modality, and polarity. While planets are the actors of the story, the zodiac tells us what those characters are wearing, how they are behaving, and what motivates them. Capricorn is the only member of the zodiac that is two distinct animals fused together, which suggests a complex relationship or hidden knowledge in the human psyche. Capricorn's catchphrase is "I utilize." Capricorn's temperament is cold and dry, perhaps bitter and old but softening with old age. Capricorn is associated with the colors black, dark gray, drab browns, and muted greens.

If we let go of the idea of Capricorn as a person with a Capricorn Sun, we can see the Capricorn archetype in everyday life. Capricorn shows up synonymous with many familiar archetypes: the hermit, the devil, the governor, the executive, the father, the boss, the daddy, the workaholic, the mentor, the go-getter, the mountain goat, the patriarch, and the wise elder crone.

Modality: Cardinal

Cardinal signs of Aries, Cancer, Libra, and Capricorn are initiators. The cardinal signs initiate the beginning of each season, as the Sun moves into these signs at the spring/fall equinoxes and summer/winter solstices. When harnessed with skill, cardinal signs start new projects, begin new relationships, and bring an entrepreneurial spirit to everything they do. Planets in these signs have the energetic power to push us out of our comfort zone and into new, scary, exciting pursuits. When unskillfully expressed, cardinal signs may be rushed, overcommitted to every new thing, and overly forceful with their energies. Cardinal signs can get so excited to embark on a new journey that they neglect to finish anything. Earthly Capricorn is capable of moving literal and metaphorical mountains. Capricorn's cardinal energy comes out in the form of building a reputation, starting a new career or business, and the commitment to patiently climb up any winding path that leads to their goal.

Element: Earth

Earth signs of Taurus, Virgo, and Capricorn are grounded in practical, tactile reality. Earth rules the physical realm and operates through tangible form. Planets in earth signs are dependable and grounded, persevering and enduring in order to achieve. Yet, like all aspects of astrology, the earth element has negative expressions; earth can be conservative and unimaginative, rigid and possessive, unable to change directions once a goal is identified. Capricorn manifests earth power through a drive to create structure and organization, as well as a desire for public recognition and tangible rewards.

Polarity: Yin

Polarity is sometimes called "gender" in astrology texts. All fire and air zodiac signs are classified as yang, which is masculine and active, while all water and earth signs of the zodiac are yin, or feminine and receptive. Though we may interpret this polarity in a similar way to other rigid binaries, such as gender (male-female), brightness (light-dark), or even the general good-bad or right-wrong binary, the implication is more about expression as introvert or extrovert. Yin signs are internal and receptive in their expression. Water and earth hold and contain; they are introverts connected to night time, mystery, and darkness. Western society, influenced by the brute power of colonialism, highly prefers and prioritizes the external, active expressions of yang energy. Capricorn's yin qualities are often overlooked in astrology texts. The sea-goat is seen as masculine, even gendered as male, due to patriarchal values and misogyny. We see rigid, emotionally controlled, responsible, mature, teacher Capricorn and assume that this archetype must be male. We even assign Capricorn as the father of the zodiac (more on this in chapter 3, Capricorn as a Parent). Yet the archetype of Capricorn speaks to the power of earth and water, the powerful receptive elements that support and respond to, rather than express and assert.

PLANETARY FOCUS: THE SUN

The Sun is not classified as a planet, but instead as our solar system's star and one of the two luminaries that light up the sky. For the purpose of this book, we will discuss the Sun as a planet, because it functions like other planets. The Sun is certainly the best-known and most misunderstood celestial body in the current landscape of pop astrology. When someone asks, "What's your sign?" you will respond with the zodiac sign where your Sun is located; if you're reading this book, you will probably say, "I'm a Capricorn!" But you are so much more complex and dynamic than just your Sun sign. Sun sign astrology, that is, the idea that you "are" your Sun, is less than 100 years old, while the language of astrology has thousands of years of history. The natal or birth chart contains all twelve signs of the zodiac and ten planets, along with thousands of mathematical points and asteroids you may choose to include or exclude. Though your Sun is centrally important, your entire chart can tell a more accurate, complex narrative of your lived experience here on planet Earth.

The Sun is the giver of light, the luminary of the day. Humans and many other animals are awake, alert, and active when the Sun rises, and they retire to a resting place when the light shifts below the horizon. The Sun's light creates the possibility for all life on planet Earth. In modern psychological astrology, the Sun is our identity and how we perceive ourselves. The glyph or symbol for the Sun is a circle with a dot in the middle, which is also the alchemical sign for gold. This astrological symbol has remained unchanged for thousands of years; the ancient solar glyph dates back to ancient cultures in what is now Greece, Egypt, and China. It is also the primary astronomical symbol for the sun, as astrology and astronomy were the same practice until astrology was dismissed by seventeenth-century philosophers. The circle, unbroken and without a distinguishable beginning or end, is a human-created representation of the infinite universe, and the dot in the middle represents the internal light of potential, unmanifested energy. In essence, the Sun represents all possibilities and potential. In astrology, the circle represents life force, spirit, soul, or vitality.

The Sun plays the role of the shining star: the center of action, self-development, and the way our self-image operates in the world. Individuals spend their lives with a particular focus on themes related to their Sun signs, especially if other planets reside in the same sign. The Sun helps us focus our willpower for action and change. When the sun is visible in the sky, we cannot see other stars or planets. We feel the warmth of the sun, asking us to stand tall and grow toward our goals.

In ancient astrology, the Sun represents who you are becoming during your lifetime. Capricorn Suns, therefore, are *becoming* Capricorns. They are not necessarily born with inherent tenacity and stamina—usually these qualities are earned during their lifespan and become emphasized due to the events and circumstances of life as it progresses over time. Though you are your Capricorn Sun, you are also your Moon, your rising, your Mercury, and so forth. You are not defined only by your hand, or your left eye, or your genitals. You are the entirety of your body and how those parts intersect and interact with one another, now and over the course of your life.

HOW TO READ THIS BOOK

This book draws on both classical ancient astrology techniques, as well as more modern psychological interpretations of the planets and zodiac signs. While Capricorn (and particularly the Capricorn Sun's experience) will remain at the center of this book, the writing is intended to be applicable to anyone who is curious about what the archetype of Capricorn has to say. Believe it or not, we all have Capricorn in our chart! Whether or not you have natal planets in Capricorn, or a strong Capricorn influence, you can learn more about yourself through the sign of the sea-goat.

Each chapter begins with an overview of the Capricorn archetype: What is the flavor, temperature, and texture that Capricorn brings to parenthood or daily life? How would the pure archetype of Capricorn function in work or in love? Then, we dive into what motivates the Capricorn Sun or Capricorn-dominant person to act, and how they may act in different areas of life. Special attention is paid to how a Capricorn may find balance, because Capricorn energies can be utilized for growth and integrity, but shadow Capricorns can also be extremely selfish in their pursuits. Each chapter ends with some practical advice and/or affirmations for the Capricorn.

Please note that while this book focuses on the Capricorn Sun's experience, numerous factors influence how the Capricorn energy is expressed. Some Capricorn Sun people will exhibit more traits of the Moon or rising sign than their stern, achievement-oriented Sun sign. Each chapter includes a special planetary or other astrological focus to tease out some details about variety in Capricornian expression. We will explore the variation in Moon, Mercury, Venus, and Mars for those who are Capricorn Suns. These planets are considered the most impactful of personal, individual expression. If you don't know what sign your natal planets are located in, you can easily look it up with your birth time and an Internet connection, or you can work with a professional astrologer. Astrology is complex and complicated, and the way we express our natal planets changes throughout our lifetime. There is not one universal Capricorn experience. If the descriptions don't resonate with you, trust yourself and don't despair! As an astrologer, I expect practical Capricorns to be critical thinkers, so take what works and leave the rest.

This book uses they/them pronouns exclusively when describing people. Using "they" instead of "he," "she," or "he/she" is a grammatically correct way to include folks of all genders as well as keep the focus on the Capricorn's behavior rather than their gender. A note about Capricorn and gender: in many, many astrology texts, Capricorn is gendered as male. Pronouns "he" and "him" are used to describe Capricorn in his quest for achievement, as he expresses exquisite self-control. In shifting away from using gendered pronouns, I hope this book will provide more universal descriptions of the archetype in action.

CAPRICORN

as a Child

The Sun is of the nature of reason; the Moon of imagination. The Sun is knowledge; the Moon, hope and faith. The Sun is strength; the Moon relaxation. The life of man must have its solar aspect, which is action, and its lunar action, which is reflection.

—MANLY P. HALL, *THE MEDICINE OF SUN AND MOON*

Each year in mid-December, the Sun's movement into the tenth zodiac sign of Capricorn marks the winter solstice in the northern hemisphere. Declaring the beginning of winter, the Sun in Capricorn is a cold and dry light, noticeably dimmer and drearier than the Sun's light in Cancer or Leo in the sweltering heat of July. Though Capricorn season begins with the shortest day of the year, the winter solstice is when the days begin to grow longer and is thus also seen as a rebirth of the light. As the Sun moves through Capricorn, our access to sunlight on Earth slowly begins to increase.

We in the United States celebrate holidays that mark the passing of time as the Sun moves through Capricorn. Christmas celebrations have roots in the Roman pagan holiday Saturnalia, where gifts and sacrifices were offered to agricultural god Saturn. In addition, new year festivities are based on the Roman tradition of giving offerings to the deity Janus, the god of change and beginnings. Marking the passage of time with rituals is an important, often undervalued, human experience, especially in the darkness of winter.

Capricorn is ruled by Saturn, known as the Greek Kronos, god of time and cycles. Saturn brings to mind hardship, limits, blockages, delays, and responsibility. Saturn is a feared planet and perhaps for good reason. Saturn does not discipline randomly and without reason. Saturn wants us to understand the rules, structures, and boundaries, and when we disregard them we must face the Saturnian consequences.

In winter, plants die back to the ground, purging every part of their body they don't need to survive. Annual plants produce seeds during the heat and abundance of summer, and these seeds are the only part of the plant that will bring life into the next cycle. The seed is the DNA, the genetic code that determines how, where, and when this plant will come back to life. Winter is not usually a time for growth and unfurling, which require warmth and wetness; it's a time of crushing darkness, cold, and a desire to stay inside and rest. This lack of light asks us to turn inward and contemplate our relationship with shadow.

The Capricorn child is born into darkness, something feared and demonized by Western culture. But there is truth in the dark, and there is beauty in the shadows. Darkness is necessary to rest the tired soul and connect with the mystery behind what is illuminated. The child born during Capricorn season contains a seed of Capricorn's grit and determination, the bare necessities required for survival. Perseverance and commitment to follow through in spite of hardship are in the Capricorn DNA.

MOTIVATION

The Capricorn Sun is motivated to create, enforce, and follow the rules and laws of society. Cardinal signs desire movement forward, growth, and initiation of something new. With an incredible drive and energy, the Capricorn

Sun person wants to pursue a path of growth and purpose. There is no peak high enough to deter the Capricorn Sun. And yet, children do not have the kind of decision-making authority that they will obtain in later life. Childhood comes with necessary limits and rules, which can either be comforting or restrictive, but the process of gaining freedom through fulfillment of responsibilities can be very satisfying for the Capricorn kid.

Capricorn is nothing if not responsible. Who or what Capricorn Sun kids are responsible to and for may depend on any number of things, such as the placement of Saturn in the natal chart and the parenting style or environment where the child is raised. Positive attachment in early life helps the Capricorn child develop a healthy sense of ego, purpose, drive, and autonomy. However, many Capricorn children feel the influence of Saturn during childhood and experience loss, trauma and wounding that in turn emphasize the need for structure, rules, and independence in later life.

Capricorn children may be incredibly goal-oriented, serious, and focused on achievement in academics, sports, or other areas where a linear and progressive success is the goal. Capricorn children often identify goals early in life. The serious sea-goat child wishes to spend their life on a pragmatic and deliberate path to their dreams. The goals and desires may change over time, or they may identify their lifelong career by age five, but Capricorn will always be able to identify something they want and work toward it with awe-inspiring determination.

Take the singer Jordin Sparks, for example: her Sun, Mercury, Saturn, Uranus, and Neptune all in the sign of Capricorn give her a natal gift for focused achievement. Jordin participated in and won many singing competitions as a child and became the youngest person to ever win the title of American Idol in 2007. This single-minded focus on getting to be the best of the best fuels many young Capricorns.

Capricorn children thrive on a steady routine from which to grow. Methodical and practical, the Capricorn Sun enjoys predictable boundaries. The Capricorn child is one who would appreciate a strict schedule; knowing that bedtime is at the exact same time each night or that pizza is served for dinner each and every Friday gives these tykes a predictable structure to lean against.

To be fair, the Capricorn Sun will spend an entire lifetime trying to relax enough to play, have childlike wonder, and have some humor about life's sour taste. Push and push and push some more is the Capricorn Sun's natural state, but life doesn't always have to be a struggle. The Capricorn child should be instructed to pursue achievement and accolade, but also take time to smell the proverbial roses. Capricorn children should be encouraged to play, rest, and experience the pleasure of being a child. To avoid loneliness, sea-goat children need to make friends their own age and participate in groups and associations, where they can better learn about interdependence and collaboration.

A natural part of human life on Earth, especially during childhood, is relying on others for care, connection, nourishment, and protection. The Capricorn child may fear vulnerability; the instinct to get everything right the first time and achieve all goals can be extremely harsh for a young being. And though the Capricorn child may have strong opinions that they proclaim loudly, their feelings are hurt when someone disagrees or challenges their authority. Once hurt, the Capricorn child will retreat into solitude. Security is a huge driving force in everything they do.

Capricorns are process-oriented and fixed on the outcome but also determined to find the most productive, efficient way of being. There is a cardinal drive for constant improvement. While Capricorn kids of all ages might behave like mini adults, American culture may be more willing to accept the Capricorn boy, as accomplishments, strength, and seriousness are attributes we tend to assign to the male sex. However, Capricorn girls may find that their desire to build and achieve is not supported by caregivers as much as adults encourage them to be emotional, relational, and sensitive creatures.

CAPRICORN CHILD IN BALANCE

At their best, Capricorn children are curious, independent, serious, and mature. They are self-sufficient, but they seek guidance from elders; they are self-directed, but they allow input from others. They take time for themselves to play and grow.

At their worst, Capricorn children are rigid, isolated, bitter, and prone to taking on other people's responsibilities. They resent those who shirk responsibility. They are critical, fixated on winning, overly serious, and dominating.

Capricorn children are mature for their age. You may find Capricorn Suns voluntarily taking up a parental role with peers and younger siblings, or they might even parent their own parents. The Capricorn child is captivated by power and might be especially motivated by financial rewards and trophies that demonstrate their worth. Even as a youth, the Capricorn has a healthy appreciation of duty, responsibility, and work. As Capricorn children sometimes seem wise beyond their years, adults in the child's life may treat them as a peer instead of as a developing young person.

While most children are engaged in fantasy, play, and self-expression, Capricorn Sun children have interests much older than their chronological age. The Capricorn child is perhaps the most stern, pragmatic child you've ever met. Saturn-influenced Capricorn children have a reputation for being rule-followers and old souls. We may even think of Capricorn as the Benjamin Button of the zodiac; born old and serious, with increased ability to frolic and enjoy leisure time in later life. Capricorn children may prefer the company of adults, engaging in conversations about practical matters that are years beyond their age.

PLANETARY FOCUS: THE MOON

The Sun is the bright, forward-moving, conscious, and active luminary of the day; by contrast, the Moon is quiet, receptive, reflective, and focused on the felt experience. Mother Moon represents a divine, nighttime goddess in every culture, whether she is called Yemaya in Santeria tradition, Selene to the ancient Greeks, Ishtar to the Babylonians, Isis to the Egyptians, Ixchel to the Mayas, or Hina to those of Polynesian descent. The glyph or symbol for the moon is a crescent moon, instantly recognizable and familiar. The Moon is the fastest moving astrological body, circling the entire zodiac every twenty-eight days. The astrological Moon speaks to our dreams, cyclical time (such as tides and menstruation), and emotional experience. The Moon is a soft, internal creature, influenced by the ever-fluctuating pace of daily life.

Children tend to embody qualities of their natal Moon sign more than their Sun sign. The Moon placement can point to how the child experiences protection and love. The Moon's sign indicates how we like to be nourished, nurtured, and held. Qualities of the natal Capricorn Sun sign might be visible or may remain hidden until adulthood.

CAPRICORN SUN WITH A FIRE MOON (ARIES, LEO, SAGITTARIUS)

Fire Moons bring more brightness, energy, impatience, and vanity to the Capricorn Sun. The combination of fire and earth brings to mind lava flows, powerful and destructive.

Capricorn Sun with an Aries Moon
(Sun Square Moon, First Quarter Moon)

The child whose Moon is in the first sign of the zodiac is an adventurous, spontaneous firecracker! Impulsive and dominant, the Aries Moon child may speak out of turn, because they must emote immediately rather than sit with their feelings. Aries and Capricorn both initiate action, so this Sun/Moon combination will seek out opportunities to create and take action. Energy is abundant, but fire can also bring explosive heat and inflammation. ♑ Celebrity example: Canadian prime minister, Justin Trudeau (Capricorn Sun, Aries Moon, Virgo rising)

Capricorn Sun with a Leo Moon
(Sun Inconjunct Moon, Disseminating Moon)

Leo Moons are flamboyant, heart-forward, self-centered children. Combined with the Capricorn Sun, the Leo Moon child has incredible leadership potential, especially if they learn to share the stage. The child with this combination should be encouraged to find an outlet for artistic self-expression. A growing edge for this placement is to learn how to access unconditional self-love and self-worth without relying on external approval. ♑ Celebrity example: Actress Marlene Dietrich (Capricorn Sun/Mercury/Saturn/Jupiter/Mars, Leo Moon, Virgo rising)

Capricorn Sun with a Sagittarius Moon
(Sun Inconjunct Moon, Balsamic Moon)

The Sagittarius Moon kiddo wants comfort and connection through finding a truth to rely on. Truths may be sought through exploration of religious texts or esoteric ritual. Individuals with this Sun and Moon combination may seem especially wise, with a desire to distill wisdom with others. ♑ Celebrity example: Actor Anthony Hopkins (Capricorn Sun/Mercury, Sagittarius Moon, Capricorn rising)

CAPRICORN SUN WITH AN EARTH MOON (TAURUS, VIRGO, CAPRICORN)

Earth Moons may bring a more grounded, practical, responsible, and cautious nature. Double Earth luminaries can be shut down and stubborn, but they also bring sensuality and reality into the here and now.

Capricorn Sun with a Taurus Moon
(Sun Trine Moon, Waxing Gibbous Moon)

The Moon is exalted in Taurus, meaning that the individual is able to touch into emotional desires, find pleasure in the body, and express needs in order to get them met. Capricorns with a Taurus Moon might be a bit rigid or stuck trying to do everything right. Individuals with this combination should release perfectionistic tendencies and embrace the process. ♑ Celebrity example: American folk musician Odetta Holmes (Capricorn Sun/Saturn/Mercury, Taurus Moon, Aquarius rising)

Capricorn Sun with a Virgo Moon
(Sun Trine Moon, Disseminating Moon)

This combination produces a child who is intelligent and practical, yet a fussy perfectionist. Capricorn Sun and Virgo Moon individuals may find themselves with a strong desire to teach and lead others, convinced that their earthly reality is better than others'. Meticulous and a bit fearful, the service-oriented Moon in Virgo shows up with a grounded temperament, a cautious, stable approach, and a strong desire for synthesis. ♑ Celebrity example: Actress Aja Naomi King (Capricorn Sun/Jupiter, Virgo Moon)

Capricorn Sun with a Capricorn Moon
(Sun Conjunct Moon, New Moon)

The Capricorn Moon child may be unable to fully embrace the softness of childhood. A Capricorn Moon is motivated to build and sustain real human connection but may feel extremely uncomfortable with vulnerability. Those with both Capricorn Sun and Moon may feel that they must be autonomous as they make their way through life, and that they cannot or should not rely on others for their survival. The Capricorn New Moon person may experience obstacles to securing their emotional needs, making them close off even more. But the Capricorn Moon child should be encouraged to feel the feelings, acknowledge the empathy that is born from scarcity, and continue forward. ♑ Celebrity example: Composer Lin-Manuel Miranda (Capricorn Sun/ Mercury, Capricorn Moon, Aries rising)

CAPRICORN SUN WITH A WATER MOON (CANCER, SCORPIO, PISCES)

Water Moons may bring increased sensitivity, emotional fluidity, compassion, and creativity. The combination of water and earth brings to mind mud and sand. With both Sun and Moon in receptive or internal modalities, this combination has much more happening below the surface.

Capricorn Sun with a Cancer Moon (Sun Opposite Moon, Full Moon)

The Capricorn Sun born with a Cancer Moon was born within a day or two of the full moon in Cancer. The person with these placements will spend their lifetime trying to manifest tangible, external results of their labor while also tending to their desire to create a vibrant, fulfilling home and family life. Moon is at home in the sign of Cancer; Cancer Moons are incredibly perceptive though perhaps a bit moody. The Cancer Moon child can attune easily to others and may have a desire to nurture or take care of others. The child with these placements is driven to nurture the growth of others. ♑ Celebrity example: Singer Mary J. Blige (Capricorn Sun, Cancer Moon)

Capricorn Sun with a Scorpio Moon
(Sun Sextile Moon, Last Quarter or Balsamic Moon)

This combination brings out a secretive nature and a compulsion toward privacy. The Scorpio Moon child is intuitive but more likely to share their magic with one or two close confidants than a gaggle of pals. Scorpio Moon is both gifted and cursed with the ability to see what lurks below the surface, and Capricorn Sun is insistent on doing something about it. With both these internal signs, this child will thrive with more solo activities rather than team sports. ♑ Celebrity example: Author David Sedaris (Capricorn Sun/Mercury, Scorpio Moon/Neptune)

Capricorn Sun with a Pisces Moon
(Sun Sextile Moon, Crescent or First Quarter Moon)

Pisces Moon is incredibly sensitive, and almost psychic, with one foot in on this plane of reality and one foot firmly planted in another realm. Capricorn will want to shut down the emotional self, but Pisces won't allow that to happen. Intuition, dream life, and spiritual growth may be a motivation for the fishy water moon child. Though the Pisces Moon is incredibly skilled at absorbing and transmuting other people's pain, they can use Capricorn Sun's focus to learn better boundaries and self-discipline. ♑ Celebrity example: Singer Patti Smith (Capricorn Sun/Mars, Pisces Moon, Sagittarius rising)

CAPRICORN SUN WITH AN AIR MOON (GEMINI, LIBRA, AQUARIUS)

Air Moons may bring additional alertness, pragmatism, and strong capacity for critical thinking. Air and earth join forces to turn ideas into blueprints, creating new visions beyond our wildest dreams.

Capricorn Sun with a Gemini Moon (Sun Inconjunct Moon, Gibbous Moon)

Writers Junot Diaz, Haruki Murakami, and Rudyard Kipling all share this placement. Lighthearted and mutable, the Gemini Moon sea-goat makes an excellent teacher, instructor, and facilitator. Capricorn Sun grounds some of the flighty qualities of the twins, while Gemini Moon gets emotional needs and nurturing through connection. Silly humor and word play bring out the softer, playful side of this combination. ♑ Celebrity example: Comedian Jim Carrey (Capricorn Sun/Venus/Mars, Gemini Moon, Scorpio rising)

Capricorn Sun with a Libra Moon
(Sun Square Moon, Last Quarter Moon)

The Libra Moon just wants everyone to be kind and beautiful. Motivated to keep the peace, Libra Moon people might be fond of white lies to spare the feelings of those around them. Then again, Libra can be the sign of justice and liberation. Adjustment and balance are the keys to happiness and success for this placement. ♑ Celebrity example: French singer Francoise Hardy (Capricorn Sun/Mercury, Libra Moon, Virgo rising)

Capricorn Sun with an Aquarius Moon
(Sun Inconjunct Moon, Crescent Moon)

The birth of new ideals, visions, and eccentric style, the Aquarius Moon brings some futuristic magic to the sea-goat. This combination wants to start something new, build new technologies or systems of power that better serve the people. Witty and hard-working, the Capricorn-Aquarius can be overly serious at times and has a hard time knowing what to do with emotions. Beware of the "my way or the highway" rigidity. ♑ Celebrity example: Professional boxer and activist Muhammad Ali (Capricorn Sun, Aquarius Moon/Mercury/Venus, Leo rising)

James Earl Jones

To better demonstrate the Capricorn child and the emphasis of a strong Saturn, let's take a look at the iconic actor James Earl Jones. Born in Mississippi in 1931 during America's Great Depression, Jones is a triple Capricorn: Capricorn Sun, Capricorn Moon, and Capricorn rising, with additional planets Mercury and Saturn in the sign of the sea-goat. At age five, he was sent to Michigan to be raised by his maternal grandparents. He developed a severe stutter as a result of the stress and trauma of moving, and as a child refused to speak. He was essentially mute for eight to ten years, not speaking to anyone other than close family. As a teenager, he had a teacher who helped him develop his voice through writing, poetry, and acting. In college he studied acting and went on to become one of the greatest actors in American history. Jones transformed his greatest weakness into his greatest strength, winning many awards during his six-decade career, though he is best known for his iconic voice.

CAPRICORN

PRACTICAL ADVICE FOR THE CAPRICORN CHILD

You have your whole life to be the responsible adult. Spend some time enjoying simple pleasures and being alive. Put your hands in the dirt, make up a silly joke, and let go of control. Feel into your body and your emotions. Don't be afraid of the darkness that you see in yourself.

CAPRICORN

as an Adult

*Saturn symbolizes a psychic process as well as a
quality or kind of experience. He is not merely a
representative of pain, restriction, and discipline; he
is also a symbol of the psychic process, natural to all
human beings, by which an individual may utilize the
experiences of pain, restriction, and discipline as a
means for greater consciousness and fulfillment.*

—LIZ GREENE, *SATURN: A NEW LOOK AT AN OLD DEVIL*

Adulthood has no standard definition. In the biolog-
ical definition, a human or other creature reaches
adulthood when sexual maturity has taken place and
reproduction is possible. In the United States, eighteen
is the age that a person becomes a legal adult. This is true
for the majority of the world, but some countries declare a
person an adult as early as fifteen or the onset of puberty
and as late as twenty. The human brain does not completely
develop its capacity for rational decision-making until
about twenty-five years of age. Some ancient peoples whose

cultural values included astrological information believed that a person didn't become a true adult until the completion of the first Saturn return, around age twenty-eight to thirty. The Western colonizer culture associates adulthood with specific activities, such as leaving the family home to pursue education and work opportunities, or perhaps entering into marriage and having children. These definitions are flawed; cultural and economic differences mean that adult life at eighteen and beyond is extremely varied.

The very notion of "adulting" was invented by and for millennials, particularly the Capricorn stellium generation. The concept of adult as a verb, a thing to be done rather than an age, is just as preposterous as assuming every eighteen-year-old has the ability to manage their own life that they did not have at age seventeen. Adulting is a way to describe the boring, mundane tasks associated with being responsible, such as grocery shopping or getting a routine oil change for your car. But things that involve bearing responsibility for a person or thing present a unique perspective. Responsibility is necessary for growth and development.

Adulthood is the time of life when one becomes responsible for their own choices, and thus the consequences of those choices. Don't want to wash your laundry? You certainly don't have to, but you will either have to pay someone else to do the work or you may lose friends and employment because you smell terrible. Social norms influence what is considered "adult" and what is not; Capricorn should be sure to understand their internal values before they blindly try to follow what others expect of them.

The limitations that the Capricorn often experiences in childhood are transformed into a healthy respect for time and duty in adulthood. Ruling planet Saturn is associated with old age and the end of life, so adulthood is more productive, satisfying, and fruitful than childhood. Saturn rules death, disease, and maturation. Though Saturn is often gendered as male, the archetype of the wrinkled crone is appropriate here, the ancient wise woman who is secure in her inner power though the outer power of beauty has diminished.

Because of the connection with Saturn, Capricorn is solid. In medical astrology traditions, the sign of Capricorn rules the skeletal system, the spine, and connective tissues; in effect, everything that holds us together. Capricorn is also said to have a special affinity for the knees "which must bend in humility" according to medical astrology texts. Preventive care for the knees, bones, teeth, and joints should be a special focus for the Capricorn adult.

PLANETARY FOCUS: SATURN

The myth of Saturn or Kronos begins with Kronos castrating his own father, Uranus, and taking his place as ruler of the universe. When Kronos hears that his destiny is to be usurped by his own son, he eats his first five children with Rhea (Demeter, Hades, Hera, Hestia, and Poseidon) so he will maintain his rulership. Rhea secretly gives birth to his sixth child, Jupiter or Zeus, in a cave and leaves infant Zeus to be cared for by the nymph Amalthaea. Zeus goes on to kill his father Kronos, free his siblings, and reign as king of the gods.

Saturn is the greater malefic, the planet that is known for bringing hardship. Ancient astrologers linked Saturn with experiences of misery, pain, sorrow, grief, punishment, solitude, and loss. Saturn is associated with the Devil card in the tarot; indeed the planet of discipline is sometimes called Satan. Saturn presides over the end of December and the months of January and February, the cold, dry winter when little can grow in the northern hemisphere. Indeed, Saturn is associated with destructive and constricting qualities of life, especially in terms of agriculture and growth. A Saturn-dominant person was characterized as dark, wearing black, silent, unable to express emotion, and serious. People and things connected in some way to long-lasting perseverance were thought to be ruled by Saturn: elders, ancient practices, and long-standing cultural norms. Because of Saturn's position as an agricultural god, those who worked the land as farmers, rented or earned money from leasing land, and individuals living in bondage or slavery were associated with the rigid and unforgiving Saturn. Saturnian expressions of human illness include depression and gloom, diseases of the bones, and hardening or crystallization within the body. Conditions such as heart disease (hardening of the arteries), cysts, arthritis, and rheumatic pain are considered under

Saturn's rulership. Saturn rules most trees, and so we may think of Saturn-dominant people as the trees of their community: pillars of strength, solid and rooted in the ground, a dedicated home to other creatures and plant life.

In the modern psychological astrology tradition, Saturn is seen as a part of the human psyche. Here, Saturn represents our self-discipline, self-sufficiency, and self-respect. Saturn-dominant people may have the gift and burden of seeing the dark and painful side of life. Saturn has long been associated with darkness; there are modern astrology texts that state that Saturn is associated with those who have dark skin. This is simply racism; the idea that whiteness and lighter complexions are pure and worthy while darkness is evil is based in the history of European colonialism, which created a system of racial prejudice in order to dominate, conquer, dehumanize, and murder indigenous people.

The glyph or symbol for Saturn is the cross (representing matter) over the half circle (representing receptivity). The glyph is also associated with a sickle, which speaks to Saturn's place in ancient Roman culture as an agricultural god. We can also think of Saturn's sickle and

Saturn in our charts as a force that helps us harvest the fruit of our labor. Fruit is not harvested the same day the tree is planted, so Saturn also represents patience, time, and an ability to put in the work before expecting rewards.

Saturn is a somewhat slow-moving planet, circling the entire zodiac approximately every thirty years. Saturn cycles can illuminate the themes or topics that are pertinent to self-development and growth, bringing about opportunities to manifest, act, and define the self. Saturn cycles can also bring depression and pain, as Saturn often asks us to take responsibility in various aspects of life.

Saturn cycles are especially significant to the Capricorn Suns. Generally, astrologers study these cycles by looking at how current astrological movement interacts with an individual's natal or birth chart. For example, when Saturn in the sky circles the entire zodiac and returns to the place it was when you were born, you experience what is called the first Saturn return, around age twenty-eight to thirty. Saturn will circle the zodiac again, and around age fifty-eight to sixty, you experience the second Saturn return. The Saturn return is a period of time that will bring opportunities to wield your power and steer your life in deeply satisfying, and/or deeply frustrating, ways. These moments in the cycle help define maturity and adulthood. Life is spent integrating and learning Saturn's lessons, which are not for the faint of heart. The Capricorn Sun will find that either they work their Saturn cycles, or the Saturn cycles will work them.

MOTIVATION

Adult Capricorn is motivated by improvement. They want to mature, to grow into their own power, and to cultivate self-awareness through self-control. Adult Capricorn seeks wisdom that is the result of deep inner self-knowing. Self-awareness and self-control are motivational forces in the Capricorn's daily life. The Capricorn adult spends their life cultivating wisdom via self-reflection; looking backward to make sense of how to move forward.

Self-improvement and self-mastery are important tools of growth for the Capricorn archetype. Activities such as competitive sports, cross-training or other disciplined exercise regimens, and running races can be excellent outlets for measured self-improvement. Capricorn Sun thrives on any activities that reward the individual for creative strategies at pushing ever forward just a bit faster or writing a few more words. Unlike fire sign companions Aries and Leo, Capricorn is not interested in being the team captain. Instead, cool and measured Capricorn is the coach. Capricorn adults (unless fire-dominant or with a natal chart that says otherwise) enjoy behind-the-scenes, or shall we say pulling-the-strings, activities. The director of the play and conductor of the orchestra, Capricorn sits back and observes. When in balance, the Capricorn Sun adult encourages others to achieve their personal best and leaves no one behind.

ADULT CAPRICORN IN BALANCE

At their best, Capricorns are responsible, kind, ambitious, and able to balance when to be generous and when to be stingy.

At their worst, they are conservative, power-hoarding, emotionless robots. They may lack empathy and they may take their bitterness out on others.

Adult humans whose natal Sun is in Capricorn probably enjoy the second half of life much more than the first. Unlike most other Sun signs, Capricorns look better with age—more distinguished, self-assured, and regal. It's hard to say whether they have relaxed into a more comfortable, confident self or whether vanity has driven them to the dermatologist. In any case, Capricorns might find retirement and/or elderhood to be the best time of life.

Depression and mental anguish are not uncommon for the sea-goat. The Capricorn adult might be prone to bouts of depression, either in a cyclical manner or in an Eeyore-esque way that permeates everyday life. Grief, depression, trauma, and loss can rule the Capricorn's world well into adulthood, especially as Capricorn encounters setbacks, limitations, and the pain of failure. The Capricorn Sun is learning to wield their own inner power. Experiences of suffering and powerlessness inform the way the Capricorn Sun continues to develop during adulthood. Some Capricorn Suns may use their pain to cultivate more empathy; others may sharpen their own power in order to hurt others before they are hurt.

Capricorn symbolizes the nonstop quest for power, such as worldly power. Sea-goat Capricorns can move effortlessly up cliffs and swim with ease to the ocean floor. They cultivate the power of self-control. Capricorn is not necessarily after money or fame, but these external displays of power serve to elevate status in a capitalist society. Capricorn seeks power as freedom, not power as glory. Integrity is the ultimate endpoint for the Capricorn archetype—merging public reputation with the inner self-image, to project only ideals and realities that are true, rather than projecting false self-confidence.

The Capricorn adult can get a reputation for being uncaring and unemotional, but many Capricorn adults simply struggle to express authentic emotions. Though they feel deeply, showing true softness or rage on the outside can present a challenge—especially if they have been taught that emotions are weak and unproductive. They project a beautiful picture of a well-curated lifestyle on social media, but behind the scenes can lurk trauma, abuse, chaos, and addiction. Projecting a self-sufficient and false sense of self can be a coping mechanism for soothing the inner critic.

Capricorn adults are more likely to offer help than receive it, even when they are in pain. Though a Capricorn is a yin, internal, receptive, nonlinear sign, it is ruled by Saturn and may thus be cold and dry, a place where emotions cannot thrive. This is the place of wisdom and death, not birth and growth.

Capricorn is cautious, unlikely to risk money or use all of their vacation time in one go. The Capricorn Sun is conservative—not necessarily politically conservative but conservative with their money, time, resources, and emotions. This may seem at cross-purposes with Capricorn's desire to be the provider, the one that the entire family can lean on. Yet it is Capricorn's self-development of the ego, of being of service, and finding confidence to facilitate rather than dominate or control that is at the root of many behaviors. Capricorn differentiates power between, power over, and power within. Capricorn Suns may wield their power for social justice or they may wield power in more self-serving ways. Capricorns may have a personality based solely on what is owned or conquered. The phrase "absolute power corrupts absolutely" brings the Capricorn archetype to mind.

They may be overly ambitious and opportunistic and may be impatient in early adulthood, thinking they have earned the status of mentor and elder before it is appropriate.

Individualism is an easy trap; Capricorn-dominant folks are strong believers in individualism, and want to believe that they have the self-determination to manifest their own destiny; however, positive thinking and individual behavior cannot undo external forces of social, political, and economic oppression. The very notion that someone is solely responsible for their own successes and failures, that one should have a linear path toward greatness and achievement, is enmeshed within our current sociopolitical framework. Though Capricorn adults have a lot of choice about how they respond to their lives and can create their own realities in that sense, systems of institutional power are always operating in the background. The Capricorn adult who is born into a body that is assigned less value in our culture (that is, non-white, Indigenous, disabled, female, trans/gender nonconforming, and so forth) will struggle to assert their worth within a world that has been socialized to dehumanize them and devalue their gifts.

Michelle Obama

Michelle Obama has her natal Sun/Mercury in Capricorn, ruled by her natal Saturn in Aquarius. Born and raised on Chicago's South Side, she traced both her maternal and paternal lineage back to enslaved African Americans in the pre–Civil War American South. Bright and steady in her achievements, she graduated cum laude from Princeton University in 1985 and received her J.D. from Harvard Law School in 1988. Though she achieved the ambitious goal of becoming a lawyer, she soon realized that corporate law was not the place for her and left to pursue a career in public service. As the First Lady of the United States, she grounded her Leo Sun husband with her traditional values. Michelle Obama was praised for her classic, traditionally elegant Capricornian fashion sense, while she also faced racist attacks on her looks and critique for being too rigid or unfeminine. Her motto "When they go low, we go high" speaks to her reliable moral compass. Capricorn's influence is noticeable in her focus on individual upward mobility and respect for the political establishment.

CAPRICORN

PRACTICAL ADVICE FOR THE
CAPRICORN ADULT

Capricorn adults won't be instantly good at everything you try, but you can achieve greatness at anything with enough time, practice, energy, and commitment. Instead of becoming a teacher or mentor prematurely, you Capricorns would do well to spend your twenties, thirties, and maybe even forties learning from teachers and mentors who inspire you. Focus on your aspirations first, not just what is easy and desirable for others (i.e., parents, friends, colleagues). If you fail, you should get up and try again. You cannot predict every twist and turn of life. Stop trying so hard and simply enjoy the ride of life. Find safe paths and places to rest.

CAPRICORN

as a Parent

Spiritual growth occurs through the fulfillment of earthly responsibilities and obligations. Through being faithful to the needs of Saturn—raising a family, holding a job, keeping commitments—we learn more about life than any book can teach. If, however, we overstep our boundaries or neglect our responsibilities, then we experience the subsequent limitation. These limitations can manifest as restrictions, blockages, frustrations, crystallized conditions, unresolved fears and inhibitions.

—DOUGLAS BLOCH AND DEMETRA GEORGE,
ASTROLOGY FOR YOURSELF

The modern archetype of Capricorn is given qualities of a stern, monotonous, reality-bound individual capable of determined achievement. The serious mountain goat is depicted as all work and no play, even a workaholic. Certainly when viewed through the lens of a capitalist society that values money and work, Capricorn is seen primarily as valuable for their ability to earn and succeed. Yet there is an underlying softness to the goat.

A myth associated with the constellation of Capricornus, which is slightly different from but informed by Capricorn, is the goat and his children. A creation of the water and the earth, goat-fish Capricornus was of the sea but could move about just as easily on land. His children, also goat-fish creatures of wisdom and intellect, swam about. He brought them to land, but once they stood on the land, they lost their ability to speak, their fishtails vanished, and they became simple goats. Capricornus mourned the loss of his children; as a creation of Saturn/ Kronos, he was able to rewind time, taking his children back into the sea. Yet the children were drawn back toward land, again losing their knowledge and wisdom. Over and over Capricornus tried to warn them, tried to prevent them from shifting into regular goats, without success. Eventually, tired and heartbroken, he asked Zeus to lift him up to the heavens, where he became a constellation.

Whether or not they have their own children, Capricorn will find themselves parenting. Perhaps this comes in the form of parenting a beloved pet, houseplant, or niece/ nephew. Perhaps this looks like reparenting the self after living with unhealthy, abusive, or addicted adult caretakers while growing up. In any case, nurturing and tending to others come naturally once an authentic connection is forged with others.

BALANCED CAPRICORN PARENT

A Capricorn parent can accomplish almost anything through willpower. This superparent ideal can be rewarding or devastating for the Capricorn Sun, who wants success and achievement in everything they do. Parenting is filled with learning opportunities, where those who once felt in control of their lives descend into total unpredictable chaos during pregnancy, birth, and infancy. The sleeping and eating routines that once helped provide structure are suddenly less important than tending to the brand-new life. Like all parents, Capricorn wants to provide their baby with a better life than the one they had.

The Capricorn Sun parent may seek out advice from evidence-based, scientifically sound parenting experts. With an eye on the tried-and-true methods of raising and nurturing their young, the Capricorn parent will spend time reviewing classic parenting books from midcentury parenting gurus like Dr. Spock. Capricorn Sun's journey involves learning their own strength and ability to survive in the face of adversity, so the Capricorn may arrive at parenthood prepared for limitations. Some Capricorn Suns will have leftover scars to heal due to strife or the burden of responsibility from their own childhood. Raising kids can be healing or retraumatizing, depending on many factors.

Capricorn Suns are cool and calculating, with the desire for power and control lurking in the background. Parenting can be a double-edged sword in this respect: it may be an opportunity for the Capricorn parent to let go of control and let some play into their lives, or it can be an opportunity for the sea-goat to dominate and micromanage their child. When the impulse to pursue power comes from a place of fear, which is normal for Saturn-dominant people, the Capricorn parent can become overprotective to a fault.

The Capricorn Sun who is not a parent will still fulfill a parenting role among friends and family. But as a loner and someone with a strong work ethic, full-time parenting or raising children might not be as desirable as other opportunities for growth, such as travel or community service. Others might judge this choice, but Capricorns should act based on what their internal compass tells them, not on what others think. Even the Capricorn who stays queen party girl for life will find ways to mother her community, her siblings and family of origin, and other young folks in her life. Childless Capricorns make excellent aunties and uncles with the potential to host the best orphan holiday gatherings for those who are excluded or far away from blood family.

The Capricorn parent is dedicated to work, whether that work is inside or outside the home. Archetypical Capricorn is responsible to self and to others, to the society and the home life. The Capricorn Sun parent can provide the kind of stability that their children need to thrive, for example always picking kids up on time and attending to the children's need for a stable attachment figure. Children of a Capricorn parent may never know how much stress, anxiety, and fear was hidden just out of view. Postpartum depression could be a possibility for these overly capable individuals, and limitations of parenthood can also bring misery and pessimism.

Capricorn is the authority and is generally comfortable in positions of power. Depending on how the Capricorn parent was parented, they might see parenting as an opportunity for self-improvement or a way to bring resources into the world.

FOCUS ON CAPRICORN—CANCER POLARITY

It's worth discussing the polarity of Cancer and Capricorn in relationship to parenting. For opposite signs Cancer and Capricorn, polarity speaks to responsibility and care. In terms of constellations, Capricornus was the "gate of death" during the dead of winter, in polar opposition to Cancer, the "gate of life" during the summer solstice. Moon-ruled Cancer responds with caring, nurturing, emotional connection, and Saturn-ruled Capricorn protects those it cares about with rules and boundaries. Where Cancer tends to feelings and intuitive emotional experiences, Capricorn cares for tangible need for food and shelter. Cancer has a reputation as the zodiacal sign most likely to cry, but really Cancer is interested in nurturing the emotional waters and connections in our lives.

Cancer is cardinal (initiating) water (emotion and intuition), and thus a sign interested in bonding and parenting. Cancer rules the chest and the pericardium in medical astrology, along with the waters of the body. Cancer is skilled at holding a gentle container for another person's process. Water seeks the deepest place it can, just as Cancer lets emotions run deep. Water runs together, just as Cancer finds other water signs Pisces and Scorpio to share secrets and dreams. Watery Cancer is influenced by the lunar cycle and seeks refuge in the ocean's currents. Water takes the shape of any container it's poured into, just as lunar Cancer shows flexibility and emotional response that is far more diverse and varied than the stereotype of crying and crabbiness.

Opposite signs of the zodiac share a unique bond and similarity; though they are working the energy in different or opposite ways, Cancer and Capricorn have a lot in common.

These signs share a modality and a polarity; in this case, Capricorn and Cancer are both cardinal initiators and yin or receptive signs. In pop culture astrology, the Cancer-Capricorn duality is considered the mother-father of the zodiac; within the nuclear family model, Cancer is the stay-at-home mom, supporting the emotional and daily wants and needs of the family, while father Capricorn is responsible for the family by making money, tending to the structures and institutions of society through employment. Cancer nurtures and cares for the children and domestic life (mother) and Capricorn brings home the bacon and manages the family's wealth and status outside the home (father). However, it does not work to apply these stereotypes to all Capricorn Sun and Cancer Sun people. Not only is it inaccurate to project them as one-dimensional, it also reinforces boring stereotypes about gender and division of labor. Families are far more complex, and gender stereotypes are tired. Some mothers fill the role of strict-disciplinarian Saturn in the family structure. Some families consist of single parents and multiple generations sharing one roof, where many adults nurture kids through emotional connections and boundaries.

Yet for some, it works to put Capricorn in the place of father archetype. Though we tend to view Capricorn through the lens of misogyny, Capricorn Suns can be as gentle as they are firm. Capricorn-dominant people of all genders may enjoy playing the role of dad if and when they raise children. Providing structure, grounding, and reliable love is earth-sign parenting expressed in balance. Caring for others comes with ease for the Capricorn, but that care might look more like practical advice and lessons about respect than cuddling and verbal affirmations of love.

PRACTICAL ADVICE FOR THE CAPRICORN PARENT

Mistakes are normal for all parents. Capricorn parents have a hard time being anything less than perfect, but every parent has flaws. Your task is to figure out how to reparent yourself, perhaps by taking your child-self out for ice cream, or doing whatever activity you love the most. Demonstrate responsibility and structure for the next generation. Act from love, not fear. Tend to the softness in yourself and do not mistake it for weakness.

CAPRICORN

in Love

*Capricorn is the sign of physical expression as a whole, the perfected physical man in which all cells of the body work in unison, changing and interchanging, with perfect circulation, replacing old and wasted cells for new, and building up the perfected temple... The sun in [Capricorn] gives longevity and the promise of ripe old age. Mars is exalted in Capricorn, the inner meaning of which is **skill in action**. The moon has her "detriment" in Capricorn, denoting restricted action.*

—ALAN LEO, *THE ART OF SYNTHESIS*

The Capricorn archetype takes love seriously. In all areas of life, romance included, Capricorn is pragmatic and practical. Because of Capricorn's desire for improvement and success, matters of the heart can be viewed as a task to be accomplished, almost the same as pursuing a job or a degree. If love, relationships, or marriage are identified as a goal, Capricorn will use their dedication and perseverance to obtain that goal. But to love and to allow others to love you is a vulnerable process, one that requires letting down the walls of pretense and the appearance of perfection. Capricorn may feel unsafe or exposed while letting their guard down.

Capricorn wants to know your five-year plan before they swipe right. On the first date, Capricorn might prefer to stick to serious or traditional subjects rather than make surface connections. Their mature, sophisticated style and cool attitude can make them seem much older than their actual age, but don't be fooled, as there is always something to be improved hiding behind the sleek exterior. You may expect Capricorn to take the role of the dominant or assertive partner because they seem so confident, but they love to be pursued and fawned over as much as the next sign. The goat-fish prefers to show affection in sensible and unsentimental ways, but don't think that Capricorns are as stone cold as their outer appearance may convey. Capricorns need tenderness and a shoulder to cry on just as much as the next person. Ancient astrology gives us the god Pan as the Capricorn archetype: sexual, horny (literally and figuratively), and playful.

BALANCED CAPRICORN SUN IN LOVE

At Capricorn's best, they are strong, capable, trustworthy, and dependable. Their outward confidence matches their inner strength. They allow people to make their own mistakes and take responsibility for their own actions, without unnecessary power dynamics. They hold on to mutually beneficial relationships, lovingly keep others accountable for their mistakes, and release relationships that aren't working.

At their worst, they are controlling, mean, selfish, and judgmental. They might think they know better than everyone else, and ego prevents them from making meaningful connections. They either crave constant validation, or they are hermits who pretend to need no one. Their jealousy makes intimacy difficult, even on a platonic level.

While the pure expression of the Capricorn archetype has a difficult time with vulnerability and love, keep in mind that Capricorn Sun people contain the entire zodiac and other planetary bodies that contribute to a person's experience of love and relationships. But Capricorn Suns must also remember that love and romance are not linear, goal-oriented practices. Romance and interpersonal relationships are more than just the identification and pursuit of a goal. Capricorn folks might have an extremely hard time with the emotions that come with breakups, betrayal, and jealousy.

As an earth sign, Capricorn Suns may find it difficult to emote and may prefer to perform acts of love through practical service and gifts. To be loved by a Capricorn partner is to always have clean, laundered sheets, a packed lunch, and both necessities and creature comforts. Or perhaps the earthy Capricorn wants to receive acts of service as a tangible, practical expression of love. Capricorn can love and be loved without any difficulty or drama, but Capricorn does not want to rely on others. Part of Capricorn's growth edge is to allow vulnerability without tipping into codependence, and to allow for solitude without becoming isolated. Alone time is necessary for the Capricorn to integrate and grow. Capricorns may be more comfortable alone, or with one or two trusted comrades. Anyone romantically or intimately connected to the Capricorn Sun must be willing to let their sweet sea-goat process their deep emotions in solitude and at their own pace. The sea-goat is half fish, after all, and needs solitude and time with their dreams as much as any water sign.

Loneliness may be a plague of the Capricorn. Sometimes it's much easier for the Capricorn Sun to project an aloof, detached, almost cold energy than to warm up and attempt connection and vulnerability. Others who are seeking a noncommittal or unattached relationship might be drawn to Capricorn's steely demeanor, but they will be surprised to see how much tender emotion is lurking just below the surface. As much as they have a reputation for being a boring stick-in-the-mud with a 9 PM bedtime, Capricorn is drawn to intimacy, safety, and loving security. They just want you to know they don't need a partner. Living unattached can bring much self-actualization and growth, but it's important for Capricorns to bond and form reliable emotional connections with others.

Capricorn has high standards; they are prone to self-protection by setting their standards so high that no one could ever attain them. But Capricorn will also try to live up to their own high standards and will aim for perfection in the dating relationship.

FAMILIAL LOVE

People love to use astrology as a tool to determine the outcomes of romance and love. The answer is always more complex than matching Sun signs. Love and compatibility extend far beyond the bonds of sexual and romantic love. Humans are social, interconnected animals who feel strong love bonds with friends, immediate and extended family, coworkers, and community. Our culture values the heteronormative bond of two opposite-sex people in a monogamous relationship, living together but separate from other adults. Perhaps those two marry and have children. This is the acceptable path for some, but not for others. Capricorn is one sign that may find satisfying relationships full of pleasure, joy, and connection in platonic relationships outside of their spouse. Chosen family may be part of Capricorn's support system. Because of Capricorn's need for integrity, strong internal values that lead to certain external behaviors, it may be difficult for the Capricorn to maintain authentic vulnerability with family and friends who do not behave with integrity.

RELATIONSHIPS AS WORK

Capricorn is a natural worker and will put in the work to form a healthy relationship. Self-discipline is a much-admired and respected quality, but Capricorn may expect partners to exude the same willingness to forgo rest and relaxation for accomplishments. For example, the Capricorn Sun person might opt for a longer workday to make that overtime money or a daily exercise regimen that begins at 5 AM and then judge others who prioritize rest. The Capricorn's romantic partnership provides opportunities for compromise. Capricorn is prone to thinking their way is the best way, so therapy or other opportunities to reflect on and define values can help the Capricorn person feel confident and grounded.

Daddy Capricorn

As a Saturn-ruled sign, Capricorn has Daddy issues. In queer and kink communities, Daddies come in all genders, shapes, and sizes, but Daddy is always in charge. Daddy is the archetype of the older, wiser partner, perhaps the primary earner, and the one who sets the limits and discipline for those who aren't following the rules. As a relational species that needs boundaries in order to thrive, humans like to have limits set for them. Domination and submission within the sexual relationship is charged with arousal, and once Capricorn lets their guard down a bit, they can enjoy exploring the limitations and boundaries of the sensual and sexual experience, especially with a trusted partner. They may find satisfaction in edgeplay and challenging sexual boundaries, choosing to integrate experiences of pleasure-pain.

Of course, kink is not inherent in any planet, sign, or placement. Romantic and sexual expression are varied and diverse in ways we cannot even imagine, and the zodiac has a lot to say about the many flavors of human desire. So while some Capricorn Suns may enjoy playing the Daddy in romantic and sexual endeavors, other Capricorns Suns will tap into power dynamics with a dominant partner.

Power dynamics aside, Capricorn Suns have a reputation for being a bit prudish and traditional when it comes to sex and relationships. Many Capricorns prefer a more standard, normative approach to relationships and can be found in long-term monogamous relationships. Capricorn Sun people may be driven to marry early and solidify their relationship as part of an old-fashioned, religion-based institution, making a relationship into a concrete, tangible contract. Getting their affairs in order and proceeding the traditional way, instead of "shacking up" as an unmarried person, might be important for them; what would their elders and ancestors say about their relationship?

Capricorns are also likely to enjoy an unattached single life where they can pursue their dreams freely, so long as they can find connection and platonic intimacy among friends and family.

PLANETARY FOCUS: VENUS

Venus is the planet of relating. A person's natal Venus speaks to what they value and don't value, what they find beautiful and pleasurable, as well as what they find repulsive. In ancient astrology, Venus (or Aphrodite) is the goddess of pleasure, love, desire, connection, beauty, and fertility. Venus wants us to experience decadence, luxury, and beauty. Venus has something to say about how we decorate our homes (or leave them bare), what our favorite foods are, and our styles of dress. Venus is far above and beyond just a planet of romantic love.

The glyph or symbol for Venus is the circle with the cross of matter below it, familiarly known as the female symbol. Sun and Venus are only ever forty-eight degrees apart, meaning Venus is never more than two signs away from the Sun. Venus spends about twelve months circling the Sun and making its way across the entire zodiac. Each year you have a Venus return, meaning Venus in the sky returns to the place it was the moment you were born.

Venus in Scorpio

Venus has a natural affinity for water, where emotions can run free and deep. However, Venus in Scorpio is motivated to pursue the deepest, most intense relationships possible. Capricorn Sun with Venus in Scorpio may be more likely to play with power dynamics in relationships, exploring the taboos of society through their private sex lives. Outlets of personal expression, like art, cooking, or other ways of transforming items to release inner feelings, are healthy for folks with this placement. Addiction, secrecy, and repressed emotions can be a problem. ♑ Celebrity example with Sun in Capricorn and Venus in Scorpio: Actor Denzel Washington, actress Ava Gardner, Republican politician Ted Cruz, fashion designer Kate Spade

Venus in Sagittarius

Fire signs are the least able to maintain Venusian balance and harmony. Connection can be singularly focused, and egoistic individualism can run amok. Capricorn Sun with Venus in Sagittarius will be more spontaneous, charismatic, and freedom-seeking than your average Capricorn. This combination may be more likely to want alone time or long-distance relationships. ♑ Celebrity example with Sun in Capricorn and Venus in Sagittarius: Professional wrestler Chyna, American jazz trumpeter Chet Baker, singer-songwriter Meghan Trainor, American soul and gospel singer Merry Clayton, actor Jude Law

Venus in Capricorn

Capricorn Sun with Capricorn Venus will be slow-moving with emotions, reliable, and practical. This Sun-Venus is the picture of beautiful perfection. Love is hands-on, material, and brings sustenance. Balance and harmony are achieved slowly. Traditions must be examined and respected. This placement loves money and power and, when balanced, can put it to good use. ♑ Celebrity example with Sun in Capricorn and Venus in Capricorn: singer Elvis Presley, actress Diane Keaton, American polymath Benjamin Franklin, writer Susan Sontag, visual artist Kiki Smith

Venus in Aquarius

Venus in air sign Aquarius can connect and move about with ease. However, Venus needs to find an ability to act in loving connection, not just talk endlessly about the idea of connecting. Venus in Aquarius may like the concept or theory of love, but putting love into action may be a challenge. Besides, Aquarian Venus has higher visions to implement before settling into a monotonous relationship.

♑ Celebrity example with Sun in Capricorn and Venus in Aquarius: Actor and musician Jared Leto, Danish model Helena Christensen, songwriter and producer Phil Spector, daughter of Beyonce and Jay-Z Blue Ivy Carter, singer/musician Joanna Newsom

Venus in Pisces

Venus in Pisces softens the edges of rigid Capricorn Sun. By loving through merging, this combination is a softer, gentler version of Capricorn. Venus is exalted in Pisces, meaning that those with this placement have an easier time connecting to the idea of universal love, forgiveness, and emotional connection than Venus in other signs. There may still be the desire to disassociate away from the feelings, so Capricorn Sun should focus on bearing responsibility for the emotions as well as the responsibilities. ♑ Celebrity example with Sun in Capricorn and Venus in Pisces: British singer-songwriter Rod Stewart, singer Pat Benatar, former FLOTUS Michelle Obama, writer and poet Edgar Allan Poe.

Dolly Parton

Dolly Parton was born in 1946 with the Sun, Venus, and Mercury all in Capricorn, ruled by her Saturn and Mars in Cancer. The fourth of twelve children, she describes her upbringing as "dirt poor." Parton began singing and performing as a child, especially in the Pentecostal church, and moved from rural Tennessee to Nashville the day after she graduated high school. She met Carl Thomas Dean almost immediately upon arriving in Nashville; they were married a few years later in 1966.

Originally breaking into the public eye as a country singer and songwriter, she has become an actor, music producer, business entrepreneur, author, and advocate for causes such as childhood literacy and HIV/AIDS. Parton has remained in the public eye since the 1960s. She is not your typical Capricorn Sun; her public persona is warm and bubbly, but she is intensely private and shrewd in business. Parton never received a formal education beyond high school, yet she is smart and wildly successful. She never had children of her own, but helped raise some of her younger siblings, and her nieces and nephews call her "Aunt Granny."

Parton's relationship to her Cancer Sun husband may seem unconventional to some, but has lasted throughout her expansive career. Though her husband avoids the spotlight and prefers to stay at home while she tours the country solo, it seems to work well for her independent and driven Venus in Capricorn. In 2016, the couple renewed their marriage vows to honor their fiftieth anniversary.

PRACTICAL ADVICE FOR CAPRICORN IN LOVE

Listen: Capricorns don't have to be so hard. You don't have to try so hard. You can soften by slathering moisturizer and fragrant oils onto your skin and wrapping yourself in silk. Self-soothing and sweetness are as easy as drinking tea from flowers and taking baths with the crystals and rocks that you already have easy access to. And you can have a wild orgasm alone and/or with others. Earth signs find a great deal of pleasure located in the body. Find partners who value your secret softness as much as they value your public displays of strength and capability. Find friends who love you deeply and allow them to see your messy humanness.

CAPRICORN

at Work

The frustrating experiences which are connected with Saturn are obviously necessary as they are educational in a practical as well as psychological sense. Whether we use psychological or esoteric terminology, the basic fact remains the same: human beings do not earn free will except through self-discovery, and they do not attempt self-discovery until things become so painful that they have no other choice.

—Liz Greene, *Saturn: A New Take on an Old Devil*

Capricorn thrives at work. Old-fashioned, orderly, and prone to making and following the rules, Capricorns may be the best capitalists you know. The Capricorn archetype is a workaholic, bound to the rules and methodology of the system where they support implementation. Measured input of effort that results in external reward in the form of money, awards, or promotions thrills the Capricorn archetype. There is always room for improvement in the

Capricorn's world, and it is no different in their work. This archetype strives for achievement and accomplishment, and thrives in later life as a teacher, mentor, or CEO. There is no room for emotions or weakness in the Capricorn's work life.

If there is one aspect of life where Capricorn thrives in the struggles, accomplishments, and achievements most, it's at work. Capricorn loves to work. The Capricorn archetype is practically synonymous with work. Capricorn puts in the time and effort required to succeed. They commit to the hard work, whether or not they receive any recognition. Capricorn must be thoughtful about becoming too attached to their work and becoming a workaholic. Capricorn can envision the outcome, then perfectly execute their plans and pursue the goal at a slow, steady pace. They are truly able to accomplish whatever they put their minds to. They know about perfectionism, but they also need to learn about interdependence.

It's easy to see Saturn's influence in the Capricorn archetype in mainstream corporate culture; you must stay within certain boundaries and follow Saturn's rules. You must limit your clothing choices, your language, your behavior, and be willing to pay close attention to time. As the god of time, Saturn (Kronos) seeks to praise those who follow the laws of the land. In our system, money is the reward for obeying and worshiping orderly, chronological time. If you disrespect Kronos by running late or something about you falls outside of the limits, punishment and boundary setting take over.

CAPRICORN AT WORK IN BALANCE

At their best, Capricorn is a leader, mentor, and honored elder. They wield power over self to set high standards, and their work's quality and integrity speak for themselves. Their self-discipline serves to keep them in line with their goals. At their worst, they are individualistic workaholics who wield power over others through fear and domination. They can be materialistic, never satisfied, and always hungry for the next prize. Their self-discipline hurts them and those around them as they neglect relationships and prioritize profits over people.

Capricorn creates tangible results. The sign of utilization and public reputation is slow and steady, bound to the earth realm, and oriented toward what is real and practical. Capricorn is the dependable taskmaster, though perhaps at times pessimistic, depressed, and gloomy, but one who can fulfill their responsibilities. The sea-goat must persevere through tedious to-do lists in order to get clarity around their sense of purpose and capability. Capricorn's journey through the work life and career will be filled with challenges, and the Capricorn's unique need is to pursue their goals even though they feel fear and insecurity. The person with a Capricorn Sun is spending their life learning the lesson of dedication and follow-through—a lesson filled with dead ends, missteps, and hardship.

However, the Capricorn Sun at work is pursuing the soul's path through determination, patience, discernment, and ambition. Capricorn sees no way around the hard work and instead plunges into the task with incredibly focused self-discipline. Perhaps it seems to the outsider that the Capricorn employee or boss always takes the long way; Capricorn may find themselves annoyed with coworkers who take shortcuts or fail to meet a deadline. Once a goal is reached, another goal is soon identified.

Though the archetype of Capricorn fits perfectly into corporate culture, the Capricorn Sun person might not. Many actors, singers, entertainers, and pop culture icons have their Sun in the sign of the sea-goat. Depending on many other factors in the chart, the Capricorn Sun may pursue accomplishments in many different fields. Capricorn finds purpose and structure within institutions, such as academia, government, or in the political/public service realm. Systems of government and businesses might be places where Capricorns flourish. But given their ability to take responsibility and build an external structure of power and influence, Capricorn Sun people can also be successful business owners and entrepreneurs. Yet Capricorn must be aware of how they wield their own power over others; be aware of corrupt behavior and hoarding of resources that often accompany access to power. Capricorn individuals should focus on wielding power over their own behavior and using self-discipline for personal development rather than meddling in the lives of others.

David Allen, a Capricorn Sun with a strong Libra influence, is an author and productivity coach who is known for creating a time management method called Getting Things Done. He is quoted as saying, "You can do anything, but not everything," which should be the mantra for Capricorn Suns all over the planet. There are limitations to our achievements, and we are more than the sum of what we achieve. Capricorn Suns must exercise patience and focus on their goals. While the Capricorn Sun is incredibly determined, they must be willing to stay with their ideas for the long haul, rather than immediately discarding the dreams that don't bring instant satisfaction.

Archetypical Capricorn wants to influence the systems that govern the world and help influence those systems of power whenever possible. Though extremely capable, Capricorn should beware of shadow expressions at work. Astrologer Steven Forrest calls Capricorn "ambitious, materialistic, power hungry . . . calculating, manipulative, quick to exploit any weakness." Indeed, when defining self-worth based solely on achievement and accomplishment, the Capricorn archetype becomes a Scrooge, capable of hurting others to achieve success. A challenge for the Capricorn at work is to deconstruct the myth of individualism.

Capricorn believes that if they just try hard enough, they can accomplish any task. However, life on planet Earth is connected, collaborative, and interdependent. Though Capricorn may believe that they don't need anyone to reach great heights, and perhaps that is true, the Capricorn Sun's life will be much less satisfying without community and relationships. Instead of sitting on a pile of hard-earned resources and money, the Capricorn person can focus on community wellness and redistribute some of their wealth.

PLANETARY FOCUS: MARS

Mars is the planet of assertion, courage, aggression, impulse, and rage. The ancient planetary force known as Mars to the Romans (and Ares to the Greeks) was a destructive and destabilizing god who ruled agriculture, military, and war. Mars in the natal chart points to our inner warrior; it speaks to how we protect ourselves when threatened. Mars needs conflict and tension, something to fight for or fight against. Mars can also be experienced as a gut reaction of desire or repulsion.

Mars takes approximately two years to travel around the entire zodiac, staying in each sign for approximately one and a half months. The glyph for Mars is the circle of spirit with an outward-focused arrow, also representing the shield and sword of the Martian warrior. This symbol is also used as the male symbol, though every person has a natal Mars that influences anger and enthusiasm.

Mars in an Earth Sign

In yin or receptive signs of earth and water, Mars has a harder time acting with impulsive courage. This can be a good thing, as is cools the temper and slows things down, but it can also bring indecisiveness. When in an earth sign, Mars has their feet planted firmly in reality. Mars wants to know: What are the real opportunities and limitations? How do we best proceed with what is here? This Mars is not interested in fantasy and play as much as completing the tasks at hand. Earth Mars can bring patience and focus to the planet of war but can also get stuck or too detail-oriented to act.

Mars in a Water Sign

Like Mars in Earth, the watery Mars is more introverted and passive. Water's sensitivity and depth can support Mars in behaving with more compassion, but it can also lead to passive-aggressive actions and communication. Mars in a water sign gives an intuitive and empathetic edge to the god of rage. Mars wants to assert the individual needs, yet water signs are extremely aware of the impact they have on others and the consequences of their behavior. Mars's energy can be unfocused and more internal than external. Art and spiritual practice may be positive outlets for those with this placement.

Mars in a Fire Sign

Mars is a hot, dry planet, and when located in the hot and dry element of fire, Mars is more competitive, aggressive, and powerful. Fiery Mars is strong, yet a strong Mars is often a destructive force in a person's life. A hot Mars is great for getting personal needs met, but they are more likely to deal with ego issues and an inflamed temper. Physical activity and an outlet for healthy competition are great ways to focus this placement.

Mars in an Air Sign

Air signs deal with connection, fluidity, and duality, which is difficult for the planet of assertion. Mars in an air sign wants to take action, whether it be fight or flight, and does not want to have to weigh multiple options or see both sides. Mars can get stuck trying to accommodate the changeable nature of air; it may be difficult to figure out which battles to fight and which battles to walk away from. People with Mars in an air sign may have many interests; they may waffle back and forth about an important decision.

Mars in Capricorn

When the natal Mars is in Capricorn, fiery hot Mars is exacting, powerful, and able to utilize its impulsiveness to pursue gut desire and exhibit bravery. However, Capricorn Mars-Sun individuals may find a need to control their anger and beware of an overinflated, power-seeking ego. Mars is exalted in the sign of Capricorn, and the planet of war finds themselves extremely strong, capable of assertion and getting stuff done. The cold/dark influence when Mars is located in Saturnian Capricorn means that the internal fire of the individual burns a little less brightly, but it gains extreme self-control and a cardinal urge for power, or the exploration of power dynamics. Aquarius Sun artist Barbara Kruger has natal Mars/Mercury in Capricorn; her work primarily consists of messages critiquing cultural constructs of power and sexual politics. Mars and Saturn are both considered malefics, or planets that bring us face-to-face with hardships, limitations, and challenges. Mars and Saturn are necessary for boundaries and self-protection.

AFFIRMATIONS FOR CAPRICORN AT WORK

♑

I don't have to do everything by myself.
Yes, I am strong and capable, but I am so much
more than what I can produce.

•

I am worthy, even when I am broke and unemployed.
I am worthy, even when I am just starting
out on a new path.

•

I connect with others in the workplace
and practice reciprocity.

CELEBRITY EXAMPLE

Jeff Bezos

Jeff Bezos, CEO and founder of Amazon, has Capricorn Sun, Mercury, and Mars, with Moon in either Sagittarius or Capricorn. He also has Saturn/Venus in Aquarius.

Mr. Bezos certainly exhibits the traits of a well-oiled Saturn machine: calculating, exacting, and driven to achieve. He embodies the Capricornian traits of self-control and shrewd decision-making, but he also seems to show the shadow side of Capricorn, which can be cruel, ruthless, and power hungry.

Mr. Bezos may be seen as a hero to some—a self-made billionaire who sits in a position of extreme wealth and power. The CEO of Amazon is one of the richest people in the world, and Amazon is slated to become the first company worth a trillion dollars in the coming years. He projects a steely, controlled exterior; he even sculpted his body from scrawny and bookish to bulked-up and buff as his company became more powerful.

Mr. Bezos is also loathed by some people and can be viewed as a villain: a rich white man hoarding wealth and power, causing mass devastation in pursuit of financial gain. The workplace environment at Amazon has been reported to be brutal and dehumanizing, especially for lower-level employees. Bezos is known to have made cruel remarks toward his staff, calling them stupid and lazy. And yet there are working-class Amazon employees who rely on food stamps and federal aid because wages are so low, job security is nonexistent, and work conditions are inhumane. Journalists have shed light on policies that discourage warehouse employees from bathroom breaks and moving slowly, as slacking off will get you fired. Yet even the success of Amazon has not been enough to quench his thirst for power—he has acquired Whole Foods, the *Washington Post*, and Blue Origin, his private "space tourism" company. Though he has caused suffering in the name of profit, in some corners he continues to be seen as a success story and continues to find new ways to dominate, colonize and "pioneer."

CAPRICORN

in School

It is true that the Sea-Goat symbolizes worldly power.
But that does not mean money. It does not mean
having your face on the cover of Newsweek. So many
seemingly powerful people live their lives as hostages,
bound by the structures of their public roles. Their
role has worldly power; they don't. And it is not the
Sea-Goat's path. For Capricorn, worldly power has a
different meaning. It does not signify glory. It signifies
freedom.

—Steven Forrest, *The Inner Sky*

Schools and systems of higher learning provide just the kind of rules, order, linear goal setting, and structure that the archetype of Capricorn appreciates. Imagine it's the first day of school and here comes Capricorn, wearing a beautifully color-coordinated back-to-school outfit, holding a stack of notebooks organized by size, and ready for the hard work that lies ahead. Though Capricorn may be neither the boldest nor smartest kid in the class, Capricorn has the gift of determination, stamina, and discipline. Hard working by nature, Capricorn will go the extra mile to achieve their goals. The Capricorn archetype enjoys setting and achieving external goals, and pursuing an advanced education is one socially accepted way to channel this impulse.

Institutions of learning themselves are very Capricornian, especially within any area of study that has at the center a theoretical framework or practical structure for organizing the chaos of the world at large: all kinds of science (political, social, physical, and health sciences), history, math, and business. Teachers and mentors exist within the realm of Capricorn.

CAPRICORN IN SCHOOL IN BALANCE

At their best, the scholarly Capricorn is a bright, hard-working, self-sufficient student who fulfills their scholarly duties. Through dedication, they can take their ideas and transform them into pragmatic bodies of work. They take responsibility for what is theirs and pay no mind to what is not. Their work elevates those around them, and they serve in leadership roles to inspire others on the path of integrity.

At their worst, the Capricorn student will do whatever it takes to succeed: lie, manipulate, and assert their power over others. While they're not much of a cheater, they are prone to interpreting rules in their favor, bending the laws to their liking, and walking away with smug self-satisfaction. They are cutthroat and will let no one stand in the way of their success.

Capricorn Suns are more likely than most to find opportunities for growth in the rigid, hierarchical structures of formal education. From elementary to advanced degrees, the Capricorn Sun student is motivated to succeed. The acquisition of knowledge beckons the Capricorn. Of course, while Capricorn is drawn to challenges, that does not mean that the challenge is easy instead of, well, challenging. In the quest for physical manifestations of personal accomplishments, Capricorn may be the type to collect degrees and academic awards. Capricorn thrives under pressure, especially when there is a goal to be attained. Determined to get a 4.0 or higher, the Capricorn Sun marches forward with incredible willpower and obedience.

The Capricorn Sun spends their entire life learning about their own capacity for self-discipline. While the other earth signs of Virgo and Taurus can identify tangible, practical goals, the Sun in those signs can let laziness or relationships get in the way of progress. Not so for Capricorn. These folks spend much of their youth growing into their solid foundations, asserting integrity with words, relationships, and action. Throughout a lifetime, the Capricorn person grows to understand how to focus their power.

CRITICAL THINKERS

Capricorn Suns may find themselves studying something practical, traditional, or in alignment with their moral philosophy on the world.

Alternative structures for education and learning may provide a different kind of challenge for the Capricorn. For example, the homeschooled or Montessori-enrolled Capricorn child may struggle with relationships more than one who receives an education in a traditional school structure. Learning environments with collaborative problem-solving or nonhierarchical models of power could be difficult for

Capricorn, whose understanding of the world is very much defined by hierarchy.

The Capricorn Sun can have a hard time when they inevitably fail. Of course, failure is not an option for the sea-goat, particularly visible and public failure. The Capricorn Sun could find themselves depressed and wallowing over an A-minus grade, because they so often define their self-worth by their external accomplishments. Capricorn Sun can do well by acknowledging and surrendering to the limitations that are beyond their control.

Defining self-worth without an external goal that can be measured and attained is challenging for the Capricorn Sun. Once schooling is complete, Capricorn could have a hard time finding a sense of self outside of formal grades and assignments. Curriculum and syllabi might not be part of everyday life, so the Capricorn Sun should use what works for them. On a personal note, I have a Capricorn Sun mother and sister, and both have gone into the teaching profession as a way to meet the need for participation in the learning environment. Capricorn Sun wants to grow into the authority on the subject.

To truly succeed, Capricorn must seek approval from within. Defining success is a deeply personal journey for Capricorn. Compelled to scale impossible mountains and achieve the very best, Capricorn will always find ways to improve. But achieving external success in areas like education can only provide so much satisfaction. The Capricorn person must be willing to do the inner work of facing their insecurities to proceed forward.

PLANETARY FOCUS: MERCURY

The planet Mercury is named after the Roman god of communication, commerce, and trade. Mercury, who is more or less synonymous with the Greek god Hermes, is the fastest-moving celestial body after the Moon. The winged messenger circles the Sun and cycles through all twelve zodiac signs roughly every eighty-eight days, with about three retrograde cycles each calendar year. The glyph for Mercury is similar to that of Venus—the circle of spirit above the cross of matter—except that Mercury also has the half-circle like a crown atop the circle, representing the winged helmet and caduceus, or staff of Hermes.

Ancient traditional astrologers prescribed a gender to every planet and sign, with the exception of Mercury, whose fluidity and dual nature are important archetypes for those who live in the gray blur between black-and-white dichotomies. Mercury is equally masculine/external and feminine/internal, equally belongs to the day and the night. Mercury rules the zodiacal signs of Virgo and Gemini, two signs that are concerned with understanding duality. Astrologer Demetra George describes ancient archetype Hermes/Mercury as guardian of the thresholds, able to travel between the conscious and unconscious worlds.

A person's natal Mercury placement speaks to their learning style, education, language skills, comprehension, and transmission of knowledge. Mercury is in charge of all types of cognitive and sensory information processing, including verbal and nonverbal communication. Mercury also rules web-based information exchange, such as social media, email, video conferencing, and emojis. Indeed, Mercury is the god of memes, the witty wordsmith, and the joker whose mouth is full of puns. Mercury flits about as a young trickster, delivering information and traveling between gods and humans, relaying gossip and important written documents. And yet Mercury also oversees travel, commerce, astrology, and alchemical magic.

Mercury travels close to the Sun, and is always within twenty-eight degrees of the Sun, meaning that Mercury will either be in the same zodiac sign as the Sun or one sign before or after the Sun. Thus those with a Sun in Capricorn will either have Mercury in Sagittarius, Capricorn, or Aquarius. The differences between a Mercury in a mutable fire, cardinal earth, or fixed air sign are quite pronounced!

Mercury in Sagittarius

Mercury is in detriment in the sign of Sagittarius, meaning that Mercury is uncomfortable and unable to do the job of exploration and communication, whimsically dancing between fantasy and reality. With Sun in Capricorn and Mercury in the sign of the centaur, the person can focus on the big picture as well as the minute details of how to accomplish grand ideas. Mercury in Sagittarius can utilize Capricorn's strong drive to direct from behind the scenes by enlisting support from others. The Mercury in Sagittarius person is able to weave tales of inspiration and will do best when given a Capricornian-organized structure to steer. This individual's learning style might be sporadic, but with the right support they can broaden the horizons for self and others. ♑ Celebrities with Capricorn Sun and Sagittarius Mercury: Puerto Rican singer Ricky Martin, songwriter and rapper Bryson Tiller, television journalist Diane Sawyer, astronomer and physicist Sir Isaac Newton, author Stephenie Meyer, professional basketball player LeBron James, actress CCH Pounder.

Mercury in Capricorn

The Capricorn Sun/Mercury person's learning style is pragmatic, normative, and traditional; perhaps the Capricorn would chose the words "classic" or "iconic" instead. Those with Sun and Mercury in Capricorn will learn and process information in a way that is slow, cautious, and focused on avoiding mistakes. Fear-based thinking can be a hurdle to overcome, as not everything has to be so serious. With a strong respect for tradition and the way things have always been done, the Sun-Mercury in Capricorn person can get so focused on practical application that communicating new ideas can be a challenge. Mercury is a flexible, inquisitive, changeable planet, but in the sign of building solid foundations, Mercury loses a bit of its flash and wonder. Capricorn-Mercury is driven to understand and maintain the status quo rather than to explore new ideas and learn from others. There is a tendency to become defensive and stubbornly cling to the way things should be if the Capricorn-Mercury's ideas are challenged or questioned. Though extremely pragmatic, the Capricorn Sun-Mercury has a hard time going with the flow or taking a joke, and these folks are even more self-critical than those with Mercury in Sagittarius or Aquarius. ♑ Celebrities with Capricorn Sun and Capricorn Mercury: TV producer and writer Shonda Rhimes, actor Taye Diggs, director Harmony Korine, singer-songwriter David Bowie, singer and actress Eartha Kitt, author J.R.R. Tolkien

Mercury in Aquarius

Mercury prefers to be in an air sign, but fixed air Aquarius, the planet of nonbinary expression can get lost in ideals.

With this combination, the Capricorn Sun provides structure and rigid form to work with, and Mercury in Aquarius dreams the larger, humanitarian visions. These folks are either rule enforcers or rule breakers. They provide stimulation to groups as they circulate among peers, spreading ideas with wild abandon. Versatile, flexible, and even more visionary than other Capricorn Sun-Mercury combinations, the learning style of Mercury in Aquarius is accelerated or unconventional. These individuals may be drawn to science and technology, or they may apply their skills at translating conventional wisdom into a modern format. ♑ Celebrities with Capricorn Sun and Aquarius Mercury: supermodel Kate Moss, American rapper Pitbull, DJ and record producer Skrillex, Dutchess of Cambridge Kate Middleton, singer-songwriter Jenny Lewis, civil rights leader Martin Luther King Jr.

Sade Adu

A Capricorn Sun with both Mercury and Saturn in Capricorn, Sade is famous for her smooth, deep voice and her musical technique that blends soft jazz, soul, reggae, Latin funk, and pop into a style that is uniquely hers. Born in Nigeria and raised in Britain by her English mother, Sade briefly worked in the fashion industry as a model and designer before she formed the band Sade and received her first record deal in 1983. Sade's first album, *Diamond Life*, and in particular the song "Smooth Operator" gained international success and catapulted her career into star territory. She sold 50 million records in the 1980s and 1990s, followed by an eight-year hiatus to raise her child.

Though her music is sometimes described as pop, the easy-listening beats overlay deep, complex emotional lyrics. Though she projects an image of the cool, beautiful Capricorn woman, we can see the influence of Saturn in her story. She is notoriously private and rarely gives interviews. Unsubstantiated rumors of her struggle with mental illness and addiction have been widespread during her career. Her family made headlines in 2016 when her child came out as a transgender man. Though she tries to keep her personal life out of the spotlight, Sade is an inspiration to other pop, hip-hop, and R&B stars like Beyoncé, Rick Ross, and Kanye West.

PRACTICAL ADVICE FOR CAPRICORN IN SCHOOL

It's okay for Capricorns to make mistakes. You should try studying something you are not inherently good at and be willing to get a lower grade without it being a calamity. You are more than an assignment, more than a theory, more than linear progression through an institution of knowledge. You are better served using your critical thinking skills to tear down the "should" than using it to beat yourself up.

CAPRICORN

in Daily Life

The goat can climb any mountain, so one of Capricorn's main issues is deciding which mountain to climb. Often the Capricornian experience is one of attaining the summit only to look around and say, "Oh, blast, wrong mountain." But from the top of even the wrong summit, often the correct one is in sight. After a momentary lapse into depression and resignation, Capricorn can then turn again to delight once the proper solo journey is mapped out in its mind. Capricorn's task is to be able to climb solitary heights where no one else can go, and to offer us a vision of what we might create together.

CAROLINE CASEY, *MAKING THE GODS WORK FOR YOU*

The Capricorn archetype is everywhere in modern Western capitalist societies. Capitalist systems frequently require the domination of marginalized people and the exploitation of their labor to benefit and enrich the business owners. Though none of us likes to face these facts, we buy and wear clothes that were made using prison labor and international child exploitation. Capitalism teaches us that those who are hard-working, self-disciplined, and rigorous in the pursuit of wealth will be rewarded with financial power. We are taught that our accomplishments and achievements are what make us powerful; people who need care, such as seniors and folks with disabilities, are seen as undesirable.

However, we know better. Systems of power and oppression operate in the background, making the rich richer and keeping the poor in poverty. Capricorn archetype can show up as the cisgender, heterosexual, white male perspective on attaining power, the individualistic corporate culture of power, and recognition behind the scenes. When we rely only on the Capricorn part of ourselves, we are encouraged to forget about or actively forgo our connection to our bodies, to one another, and to the earth. Yet the deep spiritual wisdom of the Capricorn archetype is disregarded by mainstream astrology.

Capricorn individuals grapple with how to best avoid the seduction of power and the temptation to shut off intuitive connection as they move through daily life. We must recognize that no one makes it alone. When we utilize the more

CAPRICORN

internal part of the Capricorn archetype, turning inward to face the self, we can remember our connection with the mysterious parts of life.

RELATIONSHIP BETWEEN EARTH AND WATER

In modern astrology we have reduced Capricorn to the goat—more specifically the mountain goat, whose skills and power allow ascension to the highest peaks. The mountain goat is quick-footed, calculating, and precise, running up the face of vertical cliffs with such effortlessness that we wonder if it's even difficult for the creature. But the goat association is from the mythical sea-goat of Capricorn, depicted with the head and front legs of a goat and the tail of a fish. This mythical creature is the only one in the zodiac that represents a blend of two animals. Water and earth elements are both yin, or internal polarity. The blend of these elements speaks to inner wisdom, creative potential, and unparalleled capacity for complexity. Vedic astrology associates Capricorn with the crocodile, another ancient earth-water creature.

Let us think back to the ancient god Enki, ruler of earth

(body) and water (emotion). Part of Capricorn's power is that of the dark, mysterious feminine, the yin and internal expressions. The emotional experience needs time, space, and attention for processing. Individual therapy or cultivating a relationship with a healing practitioner can be an excellent way to incorporate structured, regular space to work on giving emotions the time and attention they deserve. The body also needs regular care and attention. Reiki, massage, acupuncture, or even regular touch can help bring flow into the Capricorn's life. They should notice and care for the aches and pains of aging.

BALANCED CAPRICORN DAILY LIFE

At their best, Capricorn in daily life achieves all things in balance. Alone time feeds the Capricorn, but they must beware of unhealthy isolation. Achievement motivates the Capricorn, but they should be wary of ego-driven hoarding of wealth and resources. Capricorn thrives with a routine, but rigid structures and fear of risks can limit their brilliance. Capricorn is smart, funny, and sarcastic, but they can use their sharp wit to cut others. At their worst, Capricorn's days are filled with misery, loneliness, and suffering.

Being Saturn-ruled can be limiting and painful, but it also has its rewards. Capricorn Sun can manage productivity and time better than most and finds a natural skill for organizing, coaching, time-management, and planning. Being bound by the constraints of the world can help Capricorn feel that they fit neatly into a box, or it can be isolating.

Capricorn has a reputation for being calculating, achievement-oriented, and able to climb any mountain, but when we focus so narrowly on Capricorn's pursuit of outward growth, we miss out on what is happening internally to the sea-goat. Capricorn is wise and funny, but you must appreciate their dry, sarcastic, self-deprecating humor. Capricorn's connection to earth and water means they can read the room and act accordingly, wielding self-control over their emotions in order to practice what they preach. Capricorn is sensitive to criticism, even self-criticism that arises from within, and will go out of their way to maintain power and control over their environment.

FOCUS ON THE ASCENDANT

The rising sign, also called the ascendant, is not a planetary body or a tangible object but a calculated point that tells us which of the twelve signs of the zodiac was rising in the eastern horizon at the moment of a person's birth. This rising sign, the sign where the sky meets the earth, has important implications for how an individual meets each day. The rising sign is sometimes called the mask one wears because it shows how an individual interfaces with the world.

The rising sign is time-sensitive, changing approximately every two and a half hours. Those who do not know their birth time with some exactness may not be able to calculate their rising sign, which is not a problem. There are so many ways to interpret and understand the natal chart without a known rising sign. Individuals who are adopted, know no one who was present at their birth, or were born in locations where the birth time was not recorded accurately or at all can work with an astrologer to make a best guess of the rising sign.

CAPRICORN SUN WITH EARTH RISING

Capricorn Rising

The Capricorn Sun who is also a Capricorn rising will present a double dose of seriousness, structure, and determination. This placement brings an enormous amount of attention to the individual self, ego, and body. Internal experiences may be more visible to others and more accessible to the individual because, often, people with the same Sun/rising wear their emotions on their faces. Persons with this placement should pay special attention to preventive care for the Capricorn parts of the body, such as knees and teeth.

Taurus Rising

Taurus has a reputation for being a lazy, pleasure-oriented stick-in-the-mud, but the Taurus-rising person puts others at ease with Venusian charm. Appearing sturdy and sweet, Capricorn Sun with Taurus rising is attuned to the earth realities. This placement has a reliable temperament, providing the opportunity to become a great leader. The Sun shines brightly, making this Capricorn able to wield power in positive, productive ways for themselves and their community.

Virgo Rising

Virgo is known for their uptight, perfectionist nature. Changeable earth sign Virgo wants to categorize and sort, to critique for the purpose of better understanding. Pop-culture astrology tends to neglect to mention Virgo's role as healer, perhaps as a clinician or herbalist. Virgo thrives in the role of service to others, particularly related to health. Their critical outlook can show up as negative self-talk or an ability to thrive in academia. Artistic practice and parenthood might be places they are able to shine. They can look to the Mercury placement for additional information.

CAPRICORN SUN WITH AIR RISING

Aquarius Rising

Aquarius rising is a genius, thinking and visioning light-years ahead of their peers. Notable for their ability to bring people together, the Capricorn-Aquarius is a natural leader. However, individuals with this placement may be prone to isolation and self-loathing in private. Asserting their personal needs can feel selfish in a world of injustice, so the

Aquarian must find ways to give back to a larger community. This placement is very disciplined but it can be cold and emotionless if not balanced.

Gemini Rising

Mercury-ruled Gemini is sometimes called two-faced because of its dual nature. The twins mirror each other, so Gemini rising can easily mimic what they see. Shadow Capricorn qualities like ego and jealousy might lurk in the distance, unsure how to express fully. They can blend into many different groups and places, charming the pants off of whomever they please. Individuals with this placement may also have a strong interest in the occult, death and dying, or the greater mysteries of life on earth. Quick and clever, they shouldn't be afraid to show some of their darkness as an authentic experience.

Libra Rising

Venus-ruled Libra makes a pleasant outward-facing Capricorn who experiences the majority of their pain inwardly.

Deep-seated ancestral grief and self-loathing sit below the surface, demanding care. Individuals with this placement need to tend to their inner experience and heal their gnawing, hidden drive for power. Better to release their shadow in therapeutic or other relationships than let the shadow self-fester. Look to the natal Venus placement for additional information.

CAPRICORN SUN WITH FIRE RISING

Aries Rising

The Capricorn Sun with an Aries rising wants to assert their will and dive head-first into life. Powerful and ambitious, these folks spend much of their lives focused on career and work in the outside world. It's likely that the ram-goat will find themselves in the public world—as politicians or in world leadership. To find balance, they should focus on cultivating empathy for others and understanding that not everyone is motivated by the same urgency. Look to the Mars placement for additional information.

Leo Rising

Leo rising greets the day with a smile and a hair toss. The warm, fiery glow of lion energy can brighten the drab and serious parts of the Capricorn Sun's expression. This placement brings out the taskmaster in those capable of meeting deadlines and juggling multiple priorities while projecting warm confidence. Individuals with this placement should watch out for burnout. Prioritizing rest and self-care may not come easily, but setting some limits will help prevent exhaustion.

Sagittarius Rising

Combining the adventurous Sagittarius and the conservative Capricorn energies can bring about a bit of an identity crisis. The centaur is known for being loud, boastful, and fun, if a bit flighty and unpredictable. Individuals with this placement bring traditional values and an appreciation for hard work, which cools the impulsiveness of the Sagittarian. Money, wealth, and fine things are important to them, but a more positive, uplifted attitude can help overcome the suffering that so frequently shapes individual desires.

Pisces Rising

The Capricorn Sun with a Pisces rising exudes caring connection and can easily attune to the needs of others. Pisces rising will find some way to participate in social groups and may even find themselves working in a collective environment. Martyrdom could be a problem for these sweet and generous souls; it is much easier to give up the personal to meet the needs of work and public lives. They should pay special attention to finding balance between what is needed from others and what is needed from the self.

Cancer Rising

Cancer rising radiates kindness, empathy, and softness. Silly and sarcastic, the hard-shelled crab has a difficult time taming wild and unpredictable emotions as they arise. Ultimately, the Cancer rising shows up to care for others. The crab and the sea-goat negotiate, balancing how to care for themselves and others, including intimate partners or close friends. This placement can bring more emotional awareness and soften the hard edges of stern Capricorn.

CAPRICORN

Scorpio Rising

Dark and mysterious Scorpio rising is notoriously hard to read. Depending on the Moon and other planetary placements, the person with this placement might be interested in astrology, ritual, and the hidden forces in daily life. Capricorn Sun works hard to decode and translate, while the phoenix rising transmutes and feels into their experiences. They cultivate power in daily life through meditation, structured alone time, artistic practice, or other methods for deeper self-discovery.

PRACTICAL ADVICE FOR CAPRICORN IN DAILY LIFE

Capricorns are more than their sun sign. By studying astrology, for example by watching a quicker-moving planet such as Mercury as it transits through your natal chart, you can learn the language of the planets. (See what happens!) Learn by reading, writing, looking both forward and backward in time, and by loving your flaws, even the really annoying ones.

CAPRICORN

in the World

I believe people born with the 1988-89 Capricorn superconjunction will have a similar impact on our modern world by addressing some of our most pressing current concerns. Neptunians can be imaginative and creative. Uranians can be inventive and brilliant, thinking outside the box, especially where technology is concerned. Saturn shows the ability to persevere even when the going gets tough.

—DONNA CUNNINGHAM, *THE STELLIUM HANDBOOK*

Capricorn is the ancestor. Capricorn is the hermit. Capricorn is the wise elder; picture Dumblebore with a twinkle in his eye. Capricorn out in the world may not be the shiniest person or the star of the show, but they are the reliable, dependable one. Capricorn's cardinal energy may be pointed in the direction of world travel and exploration or toward a more traditional earth sign lifestyle of raising a family in their hometown. Astrologer Alice Sparkly Kat writes about Capricorn archetype as expressed through the Stark family of *Game of Thrones*—steely, stern, and determined to work with very little. Capricorn is from the north, where it is cold and barren. And Capricorn is patient, even when it seems hope is lost.

The United States' late-stage capitalist culture is a place where Capricorn can thrive—or be devoured. Spiritual growth and connection to something bigger than ego and money can bring peace and clarity. The American class system and values are very Capricorn—individualistic and focused on upward mobility rather than collective liberation. Capricorn can show up as shrewd nationalist policies, the way things have always been done. Capricorn can be a polite human resources worker or a sadistic boss. The Capricorn archetype shows up in the systems and structures of society, from food banks to Wall Street, from city infrastructure to hospitals. Speed limits and laws present us with rules about how to behave responsibly; for Capricorn, when we follow the rules, we get rewarded.

Capricorn commands respect out in the world. We see strong Capricorn vibes represented in presidents and

CEOs, governors and folks in charge. They are known for their ability to act with restraint, keeping information discreet when necessary. But their internal world can suffer when there is so much pressure to perform and pursue constantly. Even once they have reached the peak of recognition and success, the Capricorn might find themselves miserable. Learning how to open up and ask for help will help prevent a lonely existence.

BALANCED CAPRICORN IN THE WORLD

There are many varied ways the Capricorn Sun can shine in the world. On the one hand, Capricorn Sun Martin Luther King Jr. shaped nonviolent revolution for civil rights and anti-racism, and he continues to contribute to visions for a just future, decades after his murder. And on the other hand, Capricorn Sun Howard Hughes, who was one of the wealthiest people in his time, is best known for the end of his life as a recluse, likely suffering from a combination of addiction, mental illness, and severe obsessive-compulsive disorder. Hughes was a brilliant aviator, businessman, philanthropist, and movie producer, yet his fame and success could not prevent him from leaving a legacy as an isolated and deranged billionaire. Capricorn Suns can produce humanitarian visionaries and cutthroat corporate lone wolves, benevolent world leaders and calculating venture capitalists. When the Capricorn Sun is able to find a meaning and purpose in working for a collective cause, rather than personal gain, the Capricorn is able to best achieve a balanced approach to success.

Though Capricorn is ruled by Saturn, the Capricorn Sun does not have to find motivation through fear. Humans may dream of unlimited wishes, easy opportunities, and unencumbered living, but Saturn is here to provide boundaries and structure to all our lives. We cannot expand and grow forever. Eventually we must hit a wall, experience a rejection, or mourn a failure. These Saturnian setbacks are painful while they are happening, but they help us grow. They help us know when to give up and when to dig in with our heels.

FOCUS: OUTER PLANETS IN CAPRICORN

In astrology, Uranus, Neptune, and Pluto are called the outer planets. Unlike the personal planets Mercury, Venus, and

Mars, the outer planets in the natal or birth chart say less about the individual's personality, behavior, and identity. Outer planets speak to the larger context or slow-moving changes that happen over time, and the general qualities the individual is born into. Uranus, the great awakener, stays in each zodiac sign for eight years. Neptune, the planet of fantasy and illusion, spends roughly fourteen years in every sign. Pluto, the planet of destruction and rebirth, has an irregular orbit around the sun, so its stay in each sign can vary between fourteen and thirty-one years. A word about Pluto: though astronomers demoted Pluto's status to a dwarf planet, astrologers continue to interpret Pluto's cycles through the language of astrology, where Pluto is still considered a planet.

Uranus in Capricorn: 1988–1996

Uranus is a disruptive force and the archetype of the unconventional weirdo. Father of Zeus and king of the Titans, Uranus craves revolution. Those born under Uranus in Capricorn during the late 1980s and early 1990s share common desire to revolt, but they are limited by the traditional

Capricornian systems and structures. Though they want change, yet they must approach change restructuring what already exists, making incremental and conservative changes to the way things have always been.

Uranus in Capricorn brings the planet of authentic expression down to earth, asking those with this placement to focus on being themselves in the workplace. There may be a strong desire to revolt and disobey the rules; some of these folks have found more success in nonconventional workplaces, like driving for a ride-share company or creating their own social-media business from a strong Instagram following. Saturn-ruled Capricorn influences Uranus by bringing some structure and practical ambition to the weirdness.

Neptune in Capricorn: 1984–1998

Neptune is the dreamer and psychic connection. Roman god Neptune is comparable to Greek Poisidon, ruler of fresh water and the sea. Neptune rules our imagination and illusions, as well as our desire to dissolve the self and merge into a collective consciousness. Neptune in Capricorn speaks to the desire for or illusion of security and protection within our public institutions, though hoarding excessive wealth and fantasy of climbing to the top by any means necessary are other ways this placement can express.

The astrological generation of Neptune in Capricorn dreams of achievement, power, and high ideals perfectly executed. Those with this placement may dream of a society that functions like a well-oiled machine. Nostalgia for an imaginary and idealized past can prevent these tender souls from living in the here and now. Achieving their dreams in Capricornian ways, such as gaining status, money, and public reputation, may be a lifelong focus. Yet Neptune in Capricorn individuals might also limit their own dreams and fantasies by an approach that tends to be bitter, conservative, and realistic.

Pluto in Capricorn: 2008–2023

Pluto is a transformational, pulverizing force. Pluto, associated with Greek Hades, is the planet of creative destruction, death, and rebirth. Known as god of the underworld, Roman Pluto represents deep subconscious and purging or death of that which no longer serves us. Because of its slow movement from our perspective on Earth, Pluto's cycles speak to slow-moving, almost undetectable change in our larger society. The last time Pluto was in Capricorn (1762 to 1779), English colonizers were establishing the United States in order to gain the freedom from the oppression from the king of England. During the current Pluto in Capricorn cycle, political systems and democracy face disruption and erosion worldwide, while corruption and abuse of power have come to the surface. Business and financial structures face instability and transformation.

Those born with Pluto in Capricorn will be compelled to redefine our society's ethics, financial values, and bureaucratic structures. Individuals with this placement will carry the Pluto in Capricorn energy forward, providing opportunities to leave behind definitions of power and success that need to die and be reborn into something different. It remains to be seen exactly how this astrological generation of individuals will reinforce the adjustments made to authority, social order, success, and those in public office.

CONCLUSION

Capricorn deserves the freedom to pursue their own path. The path that works for the Capricorn may not be what works for their friends and siblings or their parents and mentors. Defining the self is a lifelong process, so Capricorns shouldn't be discouraged if they are still stumbling around in the dark. They should tend to their future ancestor selves, the part of themselves that will be humble and humorous, a grandparent type, the wise and knowing elder.

Capricorn has so many ways of expressing and wants so badly to be seen as capable. The most difficult part of the Capricorn archetype is the capacity for pain, depression, suffering, and anguish; these are the sea-goat's teachers, directing them toward what is important and away from what is frivolous. Lessons about when and how to follow the rules will always be difficult, but many of us look backward through the ups and downs of our lives and see the important lessons in the hard times. A devastating breakup can be a chance at freedom. The loss of a job gives opportunity for travel and a new career trajectory. Illness can help us slow down. No one makes it through human life unscarred, but the Capricorn can seek to find the lessons in hardship.

An individual's natal chart is a complex and beautiful thing. Looking to the natal chart gives more depth and understanding than a book about all the ways archetypes could possibly express in a person's life. Working with a professional astrologer can shed light on how individual strengths and weaknesses show up over time. As was mentioned earlier, the natal chart is somewhat static but is also moving and shifting, influenced by planetary cycles. Astrologers have different ways of interpreting the same information, so interested Capricorns should find one whose voice resonates with them. They should beware of interpretations that are actually just vaguely masked sexism, or more specifically, the idea that Capricorn men are strong and Capricorn women are bitter. Or better than seeing an astrologer for a reading, Capricorns can study astrology and learn the language themselves!

Everyone can benefit from astrology. Benjamin Franklin, J.P. Morgan, and Nancy Reagan were some unlikely advocates for astrology. Astrology can be helpful for those with a strong spiritual belief system (including mainstream religion) as well as those who are non-religious or who find a spiritual connection in nature.

A WORD ABOUT FATE VERSUS FREE WILL

Do we have control of our lives, or are our lives destined by the stars? Astrologers always want to talk about fate versus free will, whether the unfolding of human life is predetermined by outside forces or within our control, whether we should view the planets as actual forces of a higher power, and so on. I prefer analogies: astrology is the weather, and when you can predict the weather, you might be able to find out if you'll need to carry an umbrella or wear shorts. Why can't we see these outside forces as energies to work collaboratively with, instead of bending them to our will? Perhaps that's the wrong question for a book on Capricorn.

Maybe there are fated fates. Planetary condition can be determined, though modern astrologers prefer to give things a positive twist. We always have some ability to act, the capacity to make decisions that either reinforce our own worldview or dismantle it. Even within the notion of fate exists some variation. Astrologers may be able to read the general vibe, but they cannot predict with certainty the outcome of a situation. While it may be tempting to view astrology as a predictive tool, or astrologers as magical psychics who can peer into the future, it's always most helpful to pay special attention to the environment and social constructs around us. What are the planets telling us about our conditioning and our world? What can we learn by viewing things a slightly different way? Are there opportunities to see an obstacle as a gift from a place beyond our control? As a scientist, I see astrology as data collection. While the data is flawed, just like all data, it can tell us something important. And just like scientific data, astrological interpretation is somewhat subjective and influenced by sociopolitical context. Astrology as a language has survived and is now flourishing among younger generations. This is a connection back to source, back to the misunderstood and mysterious parts of human life on planet Earth.

INDEX

CAPRICORN

ABOUT THE AUTHOR

KELSEY BRANCA, MPH, is a multifaceted astrologer, writer, and facilitator. Trained as a health disparities researcher and community health worker, Kelsey believes complexity and nuance are critically important when striving for personal and collective liberation. Her work sits at the intersection of science, art, and magic. She has been a professional consulting astrologer since 2015 and her astrological approach is informed by her experience as a radical queer femme water creature, foster parent, plant-tender, and person living with chronic illness. To find out more about Kelsey and her work, visit Deepseaastrology.com.